CH00408444

Collins Illustrated Guide to

BURMA

Caroline Courtauld

COLLINS

8 Grafton Street, London W1

1988

William Collins Sons & Co. Ltd
London • Glasgow • Sydney • Auckland
Toronto • Johannesburg

British Library Cataloguing in Publication Data

Collins Illustrated Guide to Burma — (Asian Guides Series)
1. Burma — Description and Travel — Guide-books
I. Series
915.91'045   DS5273

ISBN 0-00-215262-2

First published 1988
Copyright © The Guidebook Company Ltd 1988

Series Editors: May Holdsworth and Sallie Coolidge
Picture Editor: Ingrid Morejohn

Photography by Caroline Courtauld with additional contributions by: Luca Invernizzi
Tettoni (32−33, 58−59, 63, 137, 148−149); Photobank (120, 167); Lyle Lawson (8−9,
12−13, 55, 88−89, 128−129); John Everingham (40−41, 96); Michael Freeman
(20−21); Paul Newman (84); James Montgomery (92, 190−191); Daniel Kahrs (101)

Photographs on pages 68−69, 77, courtesy of The Board of Trustees of The Victoria
and Albert Museum.

Paintings on pages 24−25, from *British Romantic Views of the First Anglo-Burmese
Wars, 1824−26* by Richard M. Cooler.

Artwork: Unity Design Studio
Maps: Bai Yiliang

Printed in Hong Kong

Contents

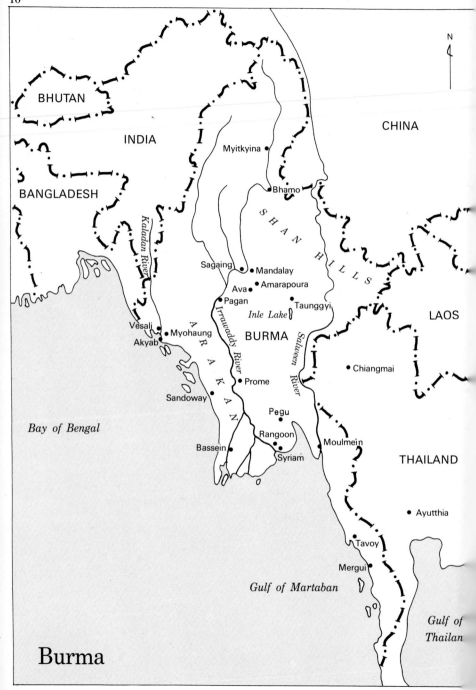

Burma

Burma

Burma is a country of a different time where time itself moves at a different speed; a country of quiet eccentricity and gentle charm, a country apart from the modern world.

To visit Burma for the seven days allowed is a delight for a genuine traveller. But the tourist who expects an air-conditioned bus to whisk him from a clinical airport to his sanitized hotel room may not find it so. Arrival at the airport is an ordeal — for an hour or so one fills in endless forms, jockeys for place, keeps hoping one's turn is next, stifles in the heat with not a single overhead fan to ruffle the air and, when one's turn comes at last, the official in his crisp white uniform gently assures one 'there's no hurry'. But for the traveller who survives this test the rewards are enormous. The moment he or she leaves the airport, whether in a relatively modern — by Burmese standards — Tourist Burma bus or a 1930s Chevrolet, a sweet soft smell pervades the air and the adventure has begun.

The drive into Rangoon, though uncomfortable, is a feast for the eye: men and women dressed elegantly in *longyis* (sarongs) go about their business; elders, sitting in front of their criss-cross mat houses, survey the scene, yellow-robed monks wander quietly along the road whilst a gang of chattering children follow behind, endlessly tying and retying their *longyis*. But the true enchantment of the country is experienced with the first glimpse of the hauntingly beautiful Shwedagon Pagoda. Its golden spire towers over the city like a glittering flame, inviting all who look to make a pilgrimage up the long stairway to its marble terraces. Kipling was right: 'This is Burma, and it will be quite unlike any land you know about.'

Sipping your rum sour, a delicious concoction of fresh lime and Mandalay rum, under the creaking fan in the Strand Hotel bar, the spell of Burmese calm will begin to work — perhaps there is more ozone in the air; more likely it is the aura of Buddhism which permeates the whole of Burmese life. One of the great charms of visiting Burma is the melting of tensions as one is inexorably drawn into the Burmese way of relaxation; even the most jaded are not exempt. Adding to this air of different calm, or rather not distracting from it, is a lack of tourists. So far Burma has not opened the flood gates to tourism, the reason given being inadequate facilities; indeed, once you have queued at the Tourist Burma office for air or rail tickets, you will know this to be the case. More fundamentally, however, the Burmese authorities have looked around at their neighbours and have witnessed the impact an influx of tourists has wrought and have opted for the time being to remain secluded.

Rangoon is a handsome city with a history of over two millennia,

though it has been a capital for a mere 100 years. Rebuilt on a grid
plan in the 1850s, the wide tree-lined boulevards are bordered by fine
stone buildings. In the 1880s Rangoon was renowned as 'Queen of the
East'. Such were her prospects, forecast the 19-century colonialist and
writer, Sir George Scott, that her trade would outstrip Calcutta before
the end of the century and 'hitherto the progress made will compare
with the most vaunted American city successes'. How wrong he proved
to be! Today Rangoon bustles without urgency, high-rise buildings,
traffic jams or department stores. Instead, small shops sell everything
from antique lacquerware and silver-backed dressing table sets, left
over from colonial days, to plastic buckets and second-hand Dorothy
L. Sayers novels. There is no forest of television antennae cluttering
up the skyline and, rather than flashy billboards proclaiming the latest
advertising slogans, there are stylish hand-painted movie posters.

Visually Burma is unique: in no other land is the eye so constantly
delighted by scenes of casual, almost unintended beauty. There is no
better way to enjoy this picture than to travel by train. Burma is an
agrarian society, and from the anonymous vantage point of your
compartment, you can absorb the essence of the country — a back-
ground of soft browns, wooden ploughs following patient oxen across
broad fields, the dazzling green paddies, noble tamarind trees and
above all, white and golden pagodas strewn across hill and field like a
cascade of jewels. Burma's chief beauty, however, lies in her people,
who exude style, grace and vivacity. Both men and women wear the
traditional *longyi* with blouse or shirt, the jet black hair of the women
often adorned with fresh flowers. The person and clothing alike are
washed obsessively often and a finishing touch to the toilette is
frequently provided by patterns of powdered, fragrant Thanaka wood
on ever-smiling faces.

The intrepid traveller will soon want to venture beyond 'metro-
politan' Rangoon. Travelling northwest on a bend of the Irrawaddy
River you discover Pagan, once capital of Burma and of the whole
Buddhist world, now an arid plain thickly studded with pagodas of all
shapes and sizes, their magnificence a testament to Pagan's former
greatness. The Irrawaddy is and always has been Burma's main artery.
Its banks have provided sites for royal capitals; boats laden with cargo
have plied the river from Bassein on the coast to Bhamo on the
Chinese border for centuries. Countless soldiers travelled her length
during the three Anglo-Burmese wars. Perhaps the most bizarre of war
vehicles was a steam vessel named Diana, a 60-horsepower paddle-
wheeler with a funnel nearly as tall as a mast. She was the first to be
used by the British forces and 'the very sight of her created more
consternation than a herd of armed elephants.'

Some 160 kilometres (100 miles) upstream from Pagan the Irrawaddy glides beneath 'the gilded spires of Mandalay and the pagoda-sprinkled heights of Sagaing.' These places, with their romantic names, have all hosted capitals, and the buildings they have to show today document their magnificent past. Of Burma's last great palace, the Gem City of Mandalay, little remains except the crenellated outer brick walls and the 70-metre (230-foot) wide moat where, 140 years ago, the royal barges, each manned by as many as 60 paddlers, floated amongst the lotus blossoms.

Southeast from Mandalay, high up on a plateau in the Shan Hills, sparkles the Inle Lake — a place of dazzling beauty and possessed of its own separate, magical quality. It is inhabited — literally, since their homes float upon the lake itself — by the Intha people renowned for their delightfully eccentric leg-rowing. Here there are no great ruins or former capitals, just breathtaking scenery; market day in Nyaung Shwe, the small town on the northern shore of the lake, is a visual delight — the costumes of the local minorities, with vibrant colours and sparkling jewellery, are, as Sir George Scott suggested, reminiscent of 'wind-stirred tulip beds or a stir about of rainbows'.

So here we have a brief glimpse of Burma as the traveller will see her, an enchanted country of enchanting people imbued with an inherent sense of style and other-worldliness. What is the source of this special Burmese timelessness? The key seems to lie in the arrival and influence of Buddhism (and in particular the Theravada form) and its interaction with Burma's geographic and ethnic circumstances.

It is easy to be misled by the apparent gentleness of this Buddhist country which however abounds in contradictions. Burma has a blood-curdling history and even today government forces are engaged with both communist insurgents and a variety of ethnic minorities seeking autonomy. There are also parallel economies — one legal, one illegal. As a visitor you will be well aware of the black market. It is hard to walk outside a tourist hotel without a furtive whisperer inviting one to change money at five to six times the official rate. But beware, the possible financial gain in comparison with the total cost of your holiday is insignificant whereas the fines are enormous and Burmese prisons best left unvisited. In fact 'black markets' themselves are no hole-in-the-corner affairs. The rows of cassette players, motor bikes and cosmetics — most smuggled in from Thailand — are displayed alongside local Shan bags, *longyis* and religious paraphernalia, without apparent embarrassment and only token police intervention.

A week is a short time but long enough to absorb and delight in some of Burma's magic and wonder at the contradictions. Relax with the Burmans in a land of untroubled acceptance of one's fate, of

making do; a land where most strive for oneness with Buddha, where, in their softness and fluidity even the colours and contours of the countryside conform to the ideals of Buddha's Middle Way; a land, to give Rudyard Kipling the last word, where 'they exist beautifully'.

General Information for Travellers

Getting to Burma

The only legal way to enter or leave Burma is via Rangoon's Mingladon Airport. Six international carriers make stops at Rangoon, with departures from Bangkok, the most convenient and popular jumping-off point (Thai Airways International, Royal Nepal Airways, Biman Bangladesh Airways and Burma Airways), Dacca (Biman), Kathmandu (Royal Nepal), Kunming (Civil Aviation Administration of China — an interesting way to enter either Burma *or* China), and perhaps the most exotic (and chancy), Aeroflot's Moscow—Tashkent—Vientiane—Rangoon loop. Burma Airways' Bangkok departure is the only daily flight. Thai International flies three times a week; the rest are weekly, and sometimes subject to cancellation (Biman is notorious in this regard).

Visas

All visitors to Burma must obtain a visa prior to departure for Rangoon. Tourist visas, good for one seven-day visit, are easily obtained at any Burmese embassy or consulate. In Bangkok it takes only 24 hours to process a tourist visa, so it is best to get your application in early in the day. Although there are frequent rumours that the visa regulations will be relaxed, extensions beyond seven days are rare.

Customs and Foreign Exchange

Burma's customs regulations and procedures are notoriously stringent. All articles of value, and many of no value, must be meticulously declared. All foreign exchange transactions must be recorded on the currency declaration form, issued upon arrival. *Do not lose this document.* Prior to departure, this form will be carefully examined to make sure that no unauthorized transactions were engaged in; calculations should show a zero balance. Further, if you are travelling independent of a group, a minimum of US$100 must be changed on arrival. This is to ensure that you have local currency during your stay.

Additional currency may exchanged at the cash counters of the Tourist Burma Hotels and Myanma Foreign Trade Bank. Unused Burmese money less the US$100 changed on arrival will be reconverted on departure. Illegal exchange of foreign currency violates the Foreign Exchange Control Regulations, which stipulate a maximum prison term of three years. Tourists are not allowed to bring in or take out local currency (*kyat*). Twelve major currencies and American Express credit cards are accepted.

One bottle of distilled spirits and one carton of cigarettes may be brought in. These items, particularly Johnny Walker whisky and 555 State Express cigarettes, make useful 'gifts'. The export of Buddha images, or any large antiques such as lacquered screens and chests, generally requires a special licence; lacking this, such items are usually confiscated at the airport, without compensation.

Health

Required (and recommended) vaccinations include: smallpox, typhoid, tetanus, cholera, and gamma globulin for hepatitis A. Burma is one of the few nations which still require presentation of the International Vaccination Certificate, and this should be brought up to date prior to departure. Although the efficacy of the cholera vaccine has been questioned, the Burmese public health authorities may refuse you entry without it. Gamma globulin is optional, but highly recommended: standards of hygiene in Burma are quite low, and hepatitis is endemic.

Malaria can be a problem anywhere in Southeast Asia, and Burma is no exception. The anti-malarial drug Fansidar, once prescribed widely for prophylaxis, has become less popular in the wake of some very serious, although rare, allergic reactions. As in all health matters pertaining to your trip, consult your doctor.

The dry, dusty conditions of the winter and early spring months can cause eye irritation. Eye drops are a must during this time of year. Aspirin, antibiotics, mosquito repellant and other first-aid items should also be packed, as they are not readily available locally.

Climate and Clothing

Burma's climate can be divided roughly into three seasons: the cool and dry season, from November to March (the best time to visit); the hot and dry season, from March to May (called 'summer' in Burma); and the rainy season, from May to October. These seasons overlay three climatic zones. The country lies mainly within the tropics; the Tropic of Cancer runs between Bhamo and Lashio some 160 kilo-

Monthly Temperatures at Mandalay and Rangoon

Mandalay

| | Temperature °F | | | | Temperature °C | | | Precipitation | |
Highest recorded	Average daily max.	min.	Lowest recorded	Highest recorded	Average daily max.	min.	Lowest recorded	Average monthly in	mm
J	91	**82**	**55**	45	33	**28**	**13**	7	0.1	3
F	99	**88**	**59**	47	37	**31**	**15**	8	0.1	3
M	108	**97**	**66**	54	42	**36**	**19**	12	0.2	5
A	110	**101**	**77**	64	43	**38**	**25**	18	1.2	31
M	111	**98**	**79**	69	44	**37**	**26**	21	5.8	147
J	107	**93**	**78**	68	42	**34**	**26**	20	6.3	160
J	106	**93**	**78**	72	41	**34**	**26**	22	2.7	69
A	101	**92**	**77**	71	38	**33**	**25**	22	4.1	104
S	103	**91**	**76**	69	39	**33**	**24**	21	5.4	137
O	102	**89**	**73**	62	39	**32**	**23**	17	4.3	109
N	98	**85**	**66**	56	37	**29**	**19**	13	2.0	51
D	90	**80**	**57**	44	32	**27**	**14**	7	0.4	10

Rangoon

| | Temperature °F | | | | Temperature °C | | | Precipitation | |
Highest recorded	Average daily max.	min.	Lowest recorded	Highest recorded	Average daily max.	min.	Lowest recorded	Average monthly in	mm
J	100	**89**	**65**	55	38	**32**	**18**	13	0.1	3
F	101	**92**	**67**	56	38	**33**	**19**	13	0.2	5
M	103	**96**	**71**	61	39	**36**	**22**	16	0.3	8
A	106	**97**	**76**	68	41	**36**	**24**	20	2.0	51
M	105	**92**	**77**	69	41	**33**	**25**	21	12.1	307
J	98	**86**	**76**	71	37	**30**	**24**	22	18.9	480
J	93	**85**	**76**	70	34	**29**	**24**	21	22.9	582
A	93	**85**	**76**	68	34	**29**	**24**	20	20.8	528
S	94	**86**	**76**	72	34	**30**	**24**	22	15.5	394
O	95	**88**	**76**	71	35	**31**	**24**	22	7.1	180
N	95	**88**	**73**	61	35	**31**	**23**	16	2.7	69
D	96	**88**	**67**	55	36	**31**	**19**	13	0.4	10

metres (100 miles) north of Mandalay. The delta area supports a typical hot, humid tropical climate, with an average rainfall of 254 centimetres (100 inches) per annum and temperatures reaching around 33°C (90°F) all year round, whereas on the Shan Plateau to the northeast temperatures drop during the cool season (November to February) to around or below freezing at night.

Generally temperatures during the cool and dry season rarely exceed 29°C (85°F) during the day, and average a pleasant 16°C (60°F) at night. The higher elevations at Maymyo and Taunggyi (Inle Lake) keep these areas considerably cooler, and clothing suitable for autumn weather in temperate latitudes (a light sweater, for instance) should be packed. Otherwise, light cotton or linen clothing is recommended. During the rainy season, a collapsible umbrella will come in handy; it is too hot for any other raingear. Formal attire will merely take up room in your suitcase; leave it at home (or in Bangkok).

During the hot and dry season, temperatures in Rangoon reach 38°C (100°F), and in Pagan daytime highs may soar to a dangerous 49°C (120°F). Light clothing, sunglasses, a hat, and a water flask are recommended. Last but not least, pack a pair of comfortable walking shoes which you can slip in and out of easily — in Burma one always removes one's shoes before entering a temple or private home.

History

Some Basic Themes Burma's history would be complex enough, but making matters even more difficult for those who try to grasp it is the fact that the country itself keeps changing shape. Kingdoms form, break up, mutate and occasionally (for three separate periods between 1056 and 1886) coalesce approximately into Burma's present-day form. 'Geography that great moulder of history' has undoubtedly been one of the key influences in Burma's development. The country is bounded on three sides by mountains and jungle and by the sea on the fourth. The peoples who migrated there found themselves in a fertile land with a clement climate. They stayed and put down roots.

This geographic insulation also served to intensify the influence of Buddhism. Its rapid acceptance as a national religion after 1056 is perhaps explained in part by the fact that Theravada Buddhism had a captive audience. It was often fervent religious belief which led the different kingdoms to split and reform: they were fighting religious wars, but for the same religion.

A fundamental theme in modern Burmese history is the impact of the West. Beginning in the 15th century Western merchants, primarily attracted by the gem trade, arrived at Burmese ports. But somehow Burma — 'tucked away on the right of the Bay of Bengal not on the way to anywhere' — never became a major trading arena. However, by the 19th century both Britain and France realized that Burma was indeed on the way to somewhere. She held the key, in the form of the Irrawaddy River, to the backdoor into China. Fear that this key might fall into the hands of the French resulted in the Third Anglo-Burmese War and, in 1886, complete absorption of Burma into the British Empire.

Early Mists Very little is known of Burma's early history and most of what information is available is hard to distinguish from the fabric of myth and legend into which it is woven. Various stone and petrified wooden implements provide evidence of men living in the Irrawaddy valley some 5,000 years ago. The major migrations began at around the beginning of the Christian era: the Mons came from present-day Thailand to settle in lower Burma; the Burmans (Mramma) grew tired of their agressive Chinese and Tibetan neighbours and fled the arid plains of southeast Tibet. The Pyus, who had in fact been at the front of this wave of migration, were pushed gradually southward by the Burmans and founded a kingdom at Srikshetra (near present-day Prome). To the west peoples from India had pushed into Arakan, where they remained until 957, when the country was overrun by Burmese and absorbed into the Kingdom of Pagan.

There are few if any documentary references to travellers visiting Burma prior to the second century BC. During his lifetime (*c.* 566–486 BC) Gautama Buddha is said to have spent a week preaching on a hill near the Arakanese city of Dhannavati (some of the city's wall can still be seen today). The story goes that at the end of Buddha's stay, his host King Candrasuriya begged him, 'Lord of Three Worlds, when you go from us we shall have no-one to whom we may pay homage. Will you not leave us the shape of yourself?' The Buddha consented — and so the Mahamuni Image (now in Mandalay) was cast by a 'heavenly sculptor'. These legendary events are minutely described in the ancient palm-leaf manuscript, *Sappadanapakarana*. Arakan also possesses a 'formal list' of kings from 2666 BC to AD 1784, that disastrous date in Arakanese history when the Mahamuni Image was taken by the Burmese. King Ashoka of India, a dedicated follower of the Buddha and convenor of the Third Buddhist Synod in 235 BC (the second had been held near Wethali in the Arakan), is thought to have visited the great Shwedagon Pagoda in Rangoon around 260 BC to pay homage to the relics of the four Buddhas interred there. Then in 128 BC the Chinese emperor Han Wu Ti sent his emissary Chang Ch'ien to Central Asia in search of new land routes to the Roman Empire. After a ten-year journey Chang Ch'ien returned to China and recommended that a route across northern Burma be opened, linking China to Bactria (the ancient country of Afghanistan). The terrain, however, made it impracticable.

The trail now goes cold although traders, and more likely Buddhist pilgrims, must have crossed northern and central Burma on their way between China and India. During the seventh and eighth centuries contemporary Chinese histories record trade between the Pyus in Lower Burma and China. There is even a description of Pyu musicians playing at the Tang Court. All this came to an abrupt end in 832 when the Pyu Kingdom was vanquished by an army from the kingdom of Nanzhao in what is today Yunnan Province in southwestern China. In the ninth century Burma's role as a corridor of trade waned as sea routes from Europe, the Middle East and India via Ceylon and the Andaman Islands to China were developed, bypassing the Burmese coastline.

The Burmese' own version of their early history (and indeed their history until 1886) is documented in the Glass Palace Chronicles. Compiled in the 19th century, this tome relies heavily on myth and legend.

First Unification In 1044 an event took place which has left an indelible stamp on Burmese history. Anawrahta, himself the son of a deposed king, seized back the Burmese throne of Pagan. Essentially a

warrior, King Anawrahta was also something of a statesman. He spent
the first few years of his reign consolidating his power, including the
defeat and absorption of his neighbouring Shan Kingdom. More
crucial still was his conversion, in 1056, to Theravada Buddhism by
Shin Arahan, a visiting monk from the court of the Mon Kingdom in
the south. Anawrahta had wearied of the Tantric spirit and animal
worship by which the original forms of Buddhism had been 'corrupted'
and took to the 'pure' Theravada form of the faith with startling zeal.
Thirsting for further knowledge, he appealed to the Mon king for a
copy of the Theravada Buddhist scriptures, the Tripitaka. When this
was not forthcoming he massed his forces and marched on Thaton.
Returning victorious, he brought back with him not only the prized
scriptures but also the Mon king Manuha himself, his White Elephant
(this is the first reference to the sacred Buddhist White Elephant), and
his entire court. With the overthrow of the Mon Kingdom, the only
other powerful domain in the region, it was the work of a few
mopping-up operations to bring the remaining petty states into line.
Thus for the first time, Burma was united into approximately its
present-day form under the guidance of a national religion. A period
of education ensued with the sophisticated southern Mons passing on
their knowledge to the northern warrior Burmese. Not only did they
provide a religion but also the script that went with it — Pali, the
written language of the Theravada texts.

This was the start of one of Burma's short excursions into
internationalism under the cloak of Buddhism. Pagan, with its proud
army of pagodas, became the world capital of Theravada Buddhism.
Anawrahta conceived the idea of a Buddhistic Empire to challenge the
doctrinal dominance of both the Indian and Chinese Buddhists. 'The
Burmese people', observes the historian, Dr Htin Aung, 'began to
consider themselves as champions of the Indo-Chinese peninsula,
whose peoples were tied to them by the silken threads of Buddhism.'
King Anawrahta made overtures to the rulers of Nanzhao and Ceylon,
possessors of the teeth of the Buddha. Not surprisingly, however, both
refused to part with their treasures and gave him copies instead.

With Buddhism King Anawrahta had given his subjects a religious
identity, but also built canals and irrigated the lands of dry Upper
Burma to ensure the production of food — much of the irrigation used
today in Upper Burma dates from his time. He died (he was gored by
a buffalo) in 1077 after a 30-year reign leaving 'a legend of power, of
religion and of authority'.

Burma remained unified for the next 200 years, due largely to
Anawrahta's statesmanship and forward thinking. Most of her energies
were devoted to Buddhism and the building of pagodas. In the middle

of the 13th century Mongol troops were moving across Asia, invading
one country after another. In 1253 they invaded Burma's northeastern
neighbour Nanzhao, and assumed that Burma would bow to their
superior military power. How wrong they were: Kublai Khan sent
several embassies to King Narathihapati of Pagan. The Burmese
answer to the first embassy was disinterest, to the second, execution of
the envoys. War was inevitable. King Narathihapati, relates Marco
Polo, 'gathered together an army of 2,000 large elephants. On each of
these was erected a wooden castle of great strength and admirably
adapted for warfare. Each of these castles was manned by at least 12
fighting men. In addition he had fully 40,000 men.' Apparently the
Khan's army was mesmerized at first by the advancing castle-adorned
elephants but, having regained their equilibrium, they showered
arrows on the unsuspecting beasts, who in turn bolted for the forest,
throwing off their hapless riders. (According to the Glass Palace
Chronicles 'the Battle of Ngasaunggyan was a furious battle, and
arrows fell so thick that even the *nat* spirits fighting on the Burmese
side were wounded.') On the return of his defeated army the king —
the master of 300 concubines and the glutton of 300 curries daily —
tore down numerous pagodas to fortify his city against the Chinese
invaders; in fact they did not invade for a further two years. The
Chinese, Marco Polo would have us believe, were an army of jugglers
and jesters from the Khan's court, although the Burmese chronicles
disagree. Before any confrontation could take place the king fled
south, thus gaining the ignominious title of Tarakpyenrin: 'the king
who ran away from the Chinese, leaving his capital to the invaders.'

Elephant Wars From the fall of Pagan until the establishment of
full British control some 600 years later Burma went through
successive periods of disintegration and reunification. On the one hand
was the persistent centrifugal force which lay behind the tendency to
split up into kingdoms based on ethnic groupings. On the other hand
was the perennial Burmese Buddhist dream of an empire comprising
essentially present-day Burma.

The religious element of the Burmese dream was the concept of
Universal Sovereign. To achieve the status of Universal Sovereign the
monarch must be in possession of the Seven Gems: The Golden
Wheel, probably the Wheel of the Law, an impression of which was on
the foot of every Buddha; the Divine Guardian of the Treasury; the
Horse; the Jewel Maiden; the Jewels that Wrought Miracles; the
General, whom it was impossible to defeat; and the seventh of these
gems, a White Elephant. 'Every Burmese king,' attests Sir George
Scott, 'longed for the capture of such a treasure during his reign as a
token that his legitimate royalty is recognised by the unseen powers.'

This was perhaps because the Buddha's final incarnation before attaining Nirvana had been, it was believed, a White Elephant. In any event the 'Lord White Elephant' played a seminal role in the wars that plagued Burma during the next hundred or so years.

The fall of Pagan in 1287 (ending the First Burmese Empire) found the various ethnic groups reforming their kingdoms. The Mons made a temporary capital at Martaban, on the east coast near their former homeland, though in 1365 they moved to Pegu (in those days a seaside port), whence they controlled Lower Burma; to the north a Shan kingdom centred on Ava was dominant and, sandwiched in between were the vanquished Burmans with their capital at Toungoo. In the west the Arakanese, always slightly removed from the mainstream, continued with their capital at Wethali until 1433 when they moved it to Mrauk-U (Myohaung). Throughout this 200-year period the Mon Kingdom at Pegu was the most powerful. It experienced a period of flourishing commerce and religious fervour. During this time the city played host to throngs of visiting monks and philosophers. During the reign of King Dhammazedi and Queen Sin Saw Bu (1453−92), the stupa of the Shwedagon Pagoda was raised to a height of 92 metres (303 feet) and gilded, for which the Queen donated her weight — a slender 40 kilograms (88 pounds) — in gold.

In 1541 the Burmese under King Tabinshweti managed to oust the Mons from Pegu and found the Second Burmese Empire. From 1550 to 1564 his successor, King Bayin-naung, was consolidating his power and wealth. Merchants, both foreign and Burmese, flocked to the newly powerful kingdom. Cesar Frederick, a Venetian, visited the great city in 1563 and reported that Bayin-naung involved himself extensively in affairs of trade and in consequence 'the King doeth take it for a most great affront to bee deceived of his Custome; ... but rubies, saphrys and spinals pay no custome in or out, because they are found growing in that countrie.' By 1564 this powerful monarch had conquered the Shan Kingdom to the north and Chiang Mai to the east. His most devastating victory was at Ayutthia, then the capital of Siam.

By 1559 the Second Burmese Empire centred at Pegu was once again in decline (though it continued to exist until 1752). King Razagyri of Arakan noted its waning power, seized his opportunity and sacked the city. He carried away not only his rival king's daughter and the treasures from Ayutthia, but also the same surviving white elephant, 'which in his eyes,' asserts Father Manrique, who visited the Arakan court in 1632, 'was of greater value than all the kingdoms of the world.' This prize enabled him to authenticate his regime by using the title 'Lord of the White Elephant' (Hsin Hpyu Shin) which he inscribed on his coins.

Arakan and its capital, Mrauk-U, or Myohaung as it is called today, now entered a brief golden era. To reach Myohaung then (as today) it was necessary to take a long boat trip through a maze of creeks. The houses stood on wooden posts, the roofs thatched with palm leaves and the walls made of bamboo matting, but 'the princes and grandees,' continues Father Manrique, 'have wooden walls to their palaces which are ornamented with carvings and gilt mouldings.'

Singuttara Hill, half a day's journey to the north of Mrauk-U, was the site of Arakan's most fabled possession, the Mahamuni Image. This statue of Buddha was supposedly cast in about 500 BC by a 'heavenly sculptor' during a visit of the Gautama Buddha to Singuttara Hill, and is said to be one of five contemporary images (of the rest, legend has it that two are in India and two in paradise!). Father Manrique describes the pomp and ceremony involved in a royal pilgrimage to the hills: the king himself travelled on a raft which was a replica of his Mrauk-U palace, and he and his court 'shimmered and glowed as they surged up the slope.' Arakan's other treasures were also shown to Father Manrique. He was led through chambers 'panelled with scented timbers such as sandalwood and eaglewood'. Father Manrique was also presented to the king's ultimate pride and joy, the Lord White Elephant. 'I can say that when he went out, even on an ordinary occasion, as in springtime to take his bath, he was conducted there under a white canopy embroidered with the insignia of royalty, and to the sound of music. Following him were servants with golden water-heaters, ewers, scrapers, and other golden utensils of the bath.'

On the death of King Thiri-thu-dhamma in 1638, and shortly thereafter, of the White Elephant, the ruin of the kingdom followed slowly but surely. A succession of weak kings, rebellions and assassinations meant that they were no match for a strong army. In 1784, the Burmese king Bodawpaya invaded Arakan, succeeded in recovering all the prizes taken by the Arkanese two centuries before and, in addition, carried away the Mahumuni Image. Throughout the centuries this image had symbolized Arakan's strength and autonomy, and with its disappearance so vanished their kingdom.

The Impact of the West The age of exploration and trade began in Europe in the 15th century. The sea routes to the East brought Italian, Portuguese, Dutch and finally British travellers and traders. In the early days when the ships had rounded the southern tip of India they hugged the coastline along the Bay of Bengal to Malaya, stopping *en route* at Burmese ports. Pegu (then a seaport) is often mentioned in contemporary traders' journals, pointing to the city's importance as a trading post.

By the mid-16th century, the Portuguese merchants, now firmly ensconced in Goa on India's western coast, proceeded to gain a foothold on Burma's Tenassarim coast. They even had a hand in helping the Burman king Tabinshweti of Toungoo overthrow the Mon king of Pegu. With their bases in Goa and Tenassarim and later at Malacca, the Portuguese were now in a position to control the sea routes round the southern tip of India across the Bay of Bengal to the Malacca Straits. An irritation with which they had not reckoned, however, was the bizarre behaviour of one of their fellow countrymen, Felipe de Brito. In 1600 his Burmese patron, King Razagyri of Arakan, sent him to become governor of the port of Syriam. He immediately fortified the town and declared Portuguese sovereignty to the satisfaction of his compatriots in Goa. But on return from a trip to Goa he both married the Viceroy's daughter, equipped himself with copious arms and ammunition and declared himself King of Syriam; such was his strength that he was able to force passing ships to come into Syriam and pay custom dues whether it was their destination or not. He is also said to have forcibly converted thousands of natives to Christianity. This situation continued for 13 years before he came to a bloody end: in 1613 Burmese laid siege to Syriam and captured the city after 34 days. 'King' de Brito was captured and impaled — it reportedly took him three days to die.

Strangely, this extraordinary episode did not seem to sour the Burmese appetite for foreign trade. In 1617 the East India Company sent their first representatives, Henry Forest and John Staveley. The king dispatched four galleons with presents to greet them. They returned to India with a letter from the king inviting English ships to Burmese ports offering free trade as an incentive.

By the mid-18th century there were French, Dutch, Portuguese and British trading posts along the southern Burmese coast. The Burmese now came into contact with the full onslaught of European diplomacy. The Mons and the Burmese were fighting their final battle for supremacy, as the French and the British were themselves fighting for dominance in the area. The French courted the Mon Kingdom. At the time the British were also negotiating with the Mons, in their case for a base at Cape Negrais (on the southern tip of the Irrawaddy delta). But neither side had foreseen the strength of the remarkable Alaungpaya, a village headman whose career began with his refusal to take the oath of allegiance to the Mons when they arrived in his small town of Shwebo. He proceeded to collect an army, march south and, to the amazement of the French and British, succeeded in ousting the Mons and provisionally set up his capital at Dagon ('end of strife'). Thus it was that the third and last Burmese Empire came into being.

The next 70 years saw the Burmese Empire expand and move capital again, this time to Amarapura, 'the City of Immortals', on the banks of the Irrawaddy. The Europeans, ever keen to secure trade agreements and access to the back-door of China, sent a succession of envoys and embassies. The Burmese enjoyed playing the game of diplomacy and (like the Chinese with the kowtow) they discovered the European Achilles' heel — 'the shoe question'. Burmese court etiquette required those attending an audience with the king to remove their shoes. Captain Michael Symes, who led the British Embassy in 1792, complied with this request but nonetheless found himself 'squatting in the audience hall, suffering from the aches and pains brought by the unnatural posture; the king and queen made a late, brief and entirely silent appearance aloft a preposterously high throne, and the envoys were allowed to watch the king chew betel and the queen smoke a huge cheroot.' Although Symes was prepared to accept such treatment, his successors were less broadminded, especially as trade agreements were not forthcoming.

Diplomatic overtures degenerated into gunboat diplomacy. King Bodawpaya, in the process of enlarging his kingdom, had captured Arakan (along with the Mahamuni Image) and had thus given Burma a common border with British India. His successor King Bagyidaw continued this expansionist policy, with frequent raids into Assam and Chittagong until, in 1824, the British were provoked into declaring war. A difficult, disease-ridden campaign followed with British troops advancing up the Irrawaddy as far as Prome. But King Bagyidaw dismissed the massive territorial concessions that were extracted from him in the subsequent treaty of Yandabo with superb nonchalance. (The British were enraged by what they considered his arrogance in the 'most grandiose fashion'.) However, there could be no doubt that their use of the Irrawaddy enabled the British forces of the East India Company to gain a decisive victory. Just 30 years later, in 1853, the two adversaries were once more locked in conflict. The outcome was the same — only this time the whole of Lower Burma was annexed by the British.

King Mindon, Burma's penultimate king, built Mandalay, the last of Burma's royal capitals, and transferred the court there in 1857. Mindon's motives in building Mandalay were both religious and secular. There was an ancient prophecy that, to mark the 2,400th anniversary of Gautama Buddha's birth, a religious centre would be built on this site and King Mindon was a deeply religious man. He was also a saddened man. By then the British had occupied half his country (the half which contained the greatest religious monument of all, the Shwedagon Pagoda, which he was never allowed to visit). He was

On their way to market, villagers disembark from an Irrawaddy ferry.

The Irrawaddy — Moulder of Burma's History

The Irrawaddy made Burma. From its source in the Eastern Himalayas the great river sweeps down from the heart of Asia to the Indian Ocean. Over the centuries deposited silt has formed the promontory of Lower Burma. For almost 1,600 kilometres (1,000 miles), from Bhamo to Bassein, the Irrawaddy is easily navigable year round and thus has formed one of the major arteries of Asia's water-borne trade.

Since the time of Buddha there have been political capitals on the river, but it was not until the 14th century that the most strategic area halfway up the Irrawaddy's navigable waters (around present-day Mandalay) was settled. Thence it was possible both to control the river highway and to guard 'the smiling fields of rice' from Chinese and Shan invaders. The early 15th century saw the advent of European traders, some of whom penetrated far up the Irrawaddy, lured by an Ava (then Burma's capital) 'in which grow rubies and many other precious stones'. However, for the next 300 years the Europeans seeking trade elsewhere were content merely to flirt with Burma.

Britain's interests in Burma were rekindled in the 1790s. By then firmly established in India, she needed to secure a steady supply of Burmese teak with which to build her ships, as well as to open up the market for her Lancashire broadcloth. When no trade agreements were reached by conventional methods, there seemed no alternative but gunboat diplomacy. Following a series of Anglo-Burmese Wars resulting in British control of Burma, the Irrawaddy came alive with activity, vessels of the Irrawaddy Flotilla Company carrying a reported nine million passengers a year, some in luxury paddlesteamers. The Company advertised that their freight included 'silk, tamarind, marble Buddhas, elephants sometimes'. Burma's riches were now sucked into British colonial trade. Teak logs lashed together and floated downriver, rice from the Irrawaddy's fertile plains, crude oil, grains, lac, sugar, tea, tobacco, and silk were exchanged for manufactured silks and worsteds, condensed milk, motor cars, corrugated iron, cutlery and, of course, sewing machines.

It was a continual source of amazement to the pre-War colonialists that the Burmese did not 'have more vigour about them' as regards material gain. An exception was Kipling who understood: 'now, if bountiful providence had put you in a pleasant damp country where rice grew of itself and fish came up to be caught, putrified and pickled, would you work?' Despite this, Burma was, prior to the Second World War, the world's largest exporter of rice. And the 'rice bowl' of Burma is the rich alluvial land of the Irrawaddy delta. This area is some 240 kilometres (150 miles) wide and 290 kilometres (180 miles) long and, it has been calculated, the deposit of silt is causing it to encroach into the Bay of Bengal at a rate of approximately five kilometres (three miles) a century — an astonishing metre (about one yard) per week.

constantly reminded of the British presence by the hoots from the Irrawaddy Flotilla Company's vessels as they plied up and down the river. So to fulfil the prophecy and as a gesture to the British of his continued potency as a monarch, he created the City of Gems.

It was for control of the Irrawaddy that a third Anglo-Burmese war was fought, in 1885. Growing French influence in the north of Burma was a source of some anxiety to the British in the south. But they were unaware of a comprehensive treaty, which included crucial shipping rights on the river, that the French were secretly negotiating with King Theebaw. In the finest Gallic tradition it was an affair of the heart which actually sparked off the war. Fanny Moroni, a Eurasian favourite at court in Mandalay and lady-in-waiting to Queen Supayalat, was also the mistress (and of course confidante) of the deputy French Consul, Monsieur Bonvilleu. Her lover compounded his indiscretions by returning to Mandalay from a spell of home leave accompanied by a new French wife. In revenge, the enraged Fanny divulged the details of the French secret plans to the British. The subsequent war consisted of a straightforward push up the Irrawaddy to Mandalay and lasted but a few months, with scant resistance from the Burmese army.

British control of Burma was now complete. The period 1890–1920 can be termed the 'golden era' of British rule. There was little bitterness on the part of the Burmese towards their British conquerers, partly because the British brought order and discipline to the country, and also because the British did not overly interfere with Burmese society as such. Though undoubtedly a considerable measure of empathy developed between the Burmese and the British, sadly they never really understood one another thoroughly. A Burmese minister is recorded to have said to a pre-colonial British envoy, 'your customs are so completely opposite in so many points. You write on white, we on black paper. You stand up, we sit down; you uncover your head, we our feet in token of respect.'

The British made one serious mistake: in the administrative structure of empire, Burma was put under the umbrella of British India and therefore made answerable to Calcutta rather than London. Given the age-old enmity between the Indians and the Burmese this was astonishingly short-sighted. To add insult to injury, in 1920 India was granted a degree of political autonomy. Burma was denied such status, being thought politically too naive. These measures sowed the seeds of the Thakin movement, which in time developed into a strong nationalist push for independence. In 1937 these efforts were rewarded when Burma was accorded separate status within the British Empire.

World War and Independence At the outbreak of the Second

World War the sympathy of the Burmese was with the British, but
they wanted to strike a bargain whereby they could aid the British in
return for dominion status after the war. However, such a promise
could not be extracted. In desperation, while the older politicians
continued to try diplomacy, Thakin Aung San, the leader of the
Thakins, and 29 other young men slipped out of the country and went
to Japan for intensive military training. Following the bombing of
Pearl Harbour on 7 December 1941, the Japanese advanced across
Southeast Asia taking Rangoon with the help of Thakin Aung San and
his '30 Comrades'.

At first the Burmese welcomed the Japanese invasion: they saw it
as liberation from colonial rule. Moreover, the Japanese promised
them independence, and they were fellow Buddhists. The Japanese
propaganda machine assured them 'the Japanese air force will respect
your pagodas, but war is war, and if your Shwedagon Pagoda is
damaged by us, we will build it anew with bricks of gold.' The
honeymoon period was short, however. Independence was not
immediately forthcoming, and individual rights basic to the Burman
were being infringed. In May 1942, a disappointed General Aung San
sent an envoy overland to India to negotiate an agreement with the
British under which his Burma Independence Army would turn and
fight against the Japanese in a combined operation. However, on the
advice of Lord Mountbatten, then Supreme Allied Commander in the
Far East (and subsequently Earl Mountbatten of Burma), General
Aung San's army of 10,000 men had to wait until March 1945 before
fighting alongside the Allies. Meanwhile, the Japanese had become
suspicious of Aung San and appointed their own officers to oversee the
Burmese army.

In Upper Burma a bloody battle raged. General 'Vinegar Joe'
Stilwell had been forced to retreat over the Western Hills to India,
losing most of his men *en route*. It was now decided that in order to
recapture Burma from the Japanese it was necessary to build a
permanent line of communication from India across to Kunming in
southwestern China, where there were Allied bases as well as those of
Chiang Kai-shek. So construction of the Ledo Road began. Some
called it the 'man-a-mile' road, owing to the immense losses from
accidents, disease and Japanese snipers. The plan was for the Ledo
Road from India to join up with the Burma Road from Mandalay and
Lashio and thence cross the mountains to Kunming. The other method
of transporting supplies from India to China was 'over the hump'.
Small planes, often badly maintained and overloaded, would weave
their way over and around the Himalayan peaks. Some 650,000 tons
were moved across the 'hump', but at a staggering cost — around

1,000 lives and 600 aircraft were lost in the process. The other key to
the eventual recovery of Burma from the Japanese was the legendary
Chindits (commandos dropped behind Japanese lines) under the
equally renowed General Wingate (see page 150). The Japanese finally
surrendered in Rangoon in May 1945, the same month that Hitler was
defeated in Europe.

The Burmese welcomed the British as liberators, not as
conquerors. But the Burmese wanted independence, and wanted it as
quickly as possible. The British colonial machine returned to Burma
for a brief three years. In London in January 1947, General Aung Sang
and the British Prime Minister Clement Atlee signed an agreement
whereby Burma was given immediate dominion status and, beginning
in 1948, total independence. At the same time her application for
membership of the newly formed United Nations was approved.
Finally she was given the option of remaining within the British
Commonwealth. On his return it was, however, decided by General
Aung San and the Constituent Assembly that Burma should not
remain in the Commonwealth. The historians' view on this point seems
to be that Burma still held two bitter memories: first, her loss of
sovereignty in 1886; and second, her unintentional involvement in the
Anglo-French rivalry of the 18th century. It was feared that to remain
within the Commonwealth would sooner or later involve Burma in
some rivalry or conflict that was not her concern. So, at dawn on 4
January 1948 Burma regained her independence and left the British
Commonwealth. General Aung San did not live to see his dream
fulfilled. He was assassinated in Rangoon, aged 32, as he and his team
were drafting the new Constitution. Thakin U Nu stepped into his
shoes and thereby became the first Prime Minister of the Union of
Burma.

Burma since Independence Economically and politically Burma
now found herself in an unhappy situation. The war had brought her
agriculture and industry to a standstill, while the post-war colonial
period had not lasted long enough to capture the benefits of stability it
had previously conferred. Furthermore the main minority groups were
fighting the new Government for autonomy. In 1948 the defeated
Chiang Kai-shek withdrew from the Chinese mainland for Taiwan.
Elements of his Kuomintang army remained on Burma's border with
Yunnan Province and were a constant source of trouble. General Ne
Win, one of the early members of the Thakin movement (and himself
of Chinese Hakka ancestry), was by now commander of Burma's
armed forces and Minister of Defence. By the mid 1950s he had
managed to contain the worst of the rebel fighting. The economy,
however, failed to improve and in 1958, ten years after independence,

Ne Win was asked to form a caretaker government. Two years later free elections were held as a result of which U Nu once again became Prime Minister. But U Nu was more interested in religion than economics: in 1956 he convened the Sixth Buddhist Synod. Notwithstanding his manifest merits and his having been an original member of the Thakin movement, U Nu was not the strongman needed to put the country back on the road to recovery, nor indeed to deal with Burma's ethnic minorities, who were once again stirring. The 1948 Constitution stated that after ten years of the Union of Burma, the principal minority groups could elect to become autonomous. But in 1962, with the economy continuing to flounder, Ne Win took control again, this time by means of a bloodless coup. Later that year a manifesto proclaiming 'The Burmese Way to Socialism' was published by the Revolutionary Council. Foreign businesses were closed, the State took control of all banks, many Chinese and Indians left, tourist visas were limited to 24 hours and the minorities' demands for autonomy were answered with military repression.

Burma's almost total seclusion continued for more than a decade. In 1974, the veil was lifted gingerly. Some foreign investment was allowed, mainly in the natural resources development field, and tourist visas were extended to seven days. In 1975 when an earthquake rocked Pagan, the Government accepted funds from the United Nations for the repairs (though all the restoration work was carried out by Burmese experts). In 1979 Ne Win withdrew Burma from the Non-Aligned Movement citing the increased influence of the Soviet Union through her proxy, Cuba. This was a surprise to the outside world but, in retrospect, seems consistent with Burma's historical determination to avoid getting caught up in others' conflicts.

Burma's tentative emergence into the outside world during the last decade has been accompanied by a quickening economic pace. In comparison to the stagnant 1950s and 1960s, however, almost any economic development would seem like a boom. Japan, the occupying power of a generation previously, has now appeared in a more constructive role, leading the way, as in so many other Southeast Asian economies, as a source of finance and a trading partner. However, travellers familiar with other non-communist countries of the region will be struck by Burma's relative lack of economic development — no glittering high-rises; no marble-lobbied hotels, virtually no modern communications or industry (nor the accompanying pollution), no international banks or other visible badges of membership of the world community of commerce. The predominance of rice is now less pronounced — Burma ceased to be the world's premier rice exporter in 1962, and teak and other hardwoods overtook rice as her largest export in 1985. Nevertheless Burma remains, as she has always been, an essentially agricultural nation. An estimated 70% of the working population is now engaged in agriculture with a further 10% in light industrial or resource-based activities such as lumber, mining and crude oil production.

While Burma is officially a socialist country, an estimated half of all economic activity takes place in the 'unofficial sector' — ranging from perfectly honest traders and entrepreneurs at one end of the spectrum, via illegal but tolerated black markets, to warlords, smugglers and drug dealers operating around Burma's borders with China, Laos and Thailand. The latter, while often written up in the international press, are most unlikely to feature in a visitor's experience of Burma. Less menacing manifestations of Burma's unofficial economy (and its interplay with the official one) are commonplace.

Low economic growth and, in consequence, very limited infrastructural development in such areas as roads and medicine are perhaps circumstances which the Burmese people will have to accept for the present. How long the country can sustain high inflation, shrinking exports and paying out some 60% of her foreign exchange earnings to repay foreign debt without radical economic reforms remains open to question. However, in late 1987 there were reports of changes in government policy, for instance the lifting of a 21-year-old ban on private trading of rice and other farm products in order to boost production. Wide-ranging economic reforms are rumoured to be introduced in the near future.

Burma's contemporary political situation is equally full of difficult questions and uncertainties. U Ne Win, although no longer President, is still Chairman of the Burma Socialist Party and, in his mid-70s, is very much at the helm. San Yu, his successor as President and also Vice-Chairman of the Burmese Socialist Party, was originally expected in time to inherit the full mantle of Ne Win's power, but he is reported to be in ill health, and the guessing game continues.

Geography

Geographically the Burmese are blessed in all respects. This country of roughly 673,500 square kilometres (260,000 square miles) is enclosed by a horseshoe formation of mountain ranges which give dual protection from invaders and the weather. Along her border with India and Bangladesh the Western Hills, an offshoot of the eastern Himalayas, form a massive wall as they swing southward in an arc through the Naga and Chin Hills to the Arakan Yoma (hills), which end just short of the Irrawaddy delta. Her northern border with China is flanked by a semi-circular continuation of the Tibetan range where even the passes are well over 3,000 metres (10,000 feet) above sea level and which boasts Southeast Asia's highest peak, Hkakabo Razi (5,920 metres or 19,296 feet). Burma's eastern border with China, Laos and Thailand is guarded by the Kachin Hills which meld into the limestone tableland of the Shan Plateau (a continuation of China's Yunnan Plateau) with an average elevation of 1,000 metres (3,000 feet); at their southern end the Kachin Hills break into parallel ranges known collectively as the Tenassarim Yomas. Down the heart of Burma, running along the Irrawaddy, are the Pegu Yomas, and it is on their southernmost spur that the great Shwedagon Pagoda stands. Within this horseshoe frame of mountains the centre is cut by four river valleys, those of the Irrawaddy, the Chindwin, the Salween and the Sittang. The Bay of Bengal marks the southern limit of the country.

In the delta region mostly rice is grown. In the rest of the country a myriad of crops abound: cotton, sesame, tea, jute, sugarcane, maize and tobacco. (Burma, observed Kipling, 'is a delightfully lazy land full of pretty girls and very bad cheroots.') This land of plenty also boasts a wealth of mineral and other natural resources: jade, emeralds, sapphires, rubies as well as a variety of semi-precious stones, tungsten, silver, copper, tin, oil and Burma's second largest export after rice, teak. Most of the teak comes from the forests in the north. There, trees are felled with the help of elephants which then drag them down to the banks of the Irrawaddy. Here they are lashed together into large log rafts on each of which perches a hut to house the captain, who pilots the craft downstream. Some will make the full journey to the sawmills of Rangoon. For others the destination will be Mandalay, where the logs are unlashed and then, trunk by trunk, hauled out of the river by water buffalo.

Fishing is one of Burma's contradictions. Buddhist philosophy says 'thou shalt not take any life'; yet fish is Burma's favourite food, so a compromise has been found: it is acceptable to buy fish (and indeed meat and poultry — butchers in Burma are predominately Muslim or

Chinese) as long as one does not actually order the animal in question to be slaughtered. So where does that leave the fisherman? He is regarded by some as the lowest category of man who will undoubtedly be banished to the 'Bong of Animals' in the next life. To others the fisherman 'is nobly drawing demerit on further reincarnations by providing the nation's favourite food.' And to his own conscience? Why, he is saving the fish from drowning! He plucks the fish from the water, laying them on the bank to recover, and if they die that is not his fault. The result of this somewhat tortuous logic seems to be that every Burmese river is peopled with fishermen. On the bank men stand knee-deep in mud, with a cylindrical basket in which to store their catch strapped on their backs. As one sails past, an object shaped like some prehistoric creature may bob to the surface: this is one of the fish traps used in deeper waters. Meanwhile, varieties of small craft move slowly across the surface of the water, a line dangling over the gunwale, the occupant dozing under his hat.

The driest area of all are the highlands which encircle and protect the country. So thick is the jungle, and so poor the soil in most of these areas, that their people (predominately Burma's ethnic minorities) are forced to lead a nomadic existence. These hill tribes still practise the *taunggya* (slash-and-burn) method of cultivation. The method of clearing a hilly site provides a pertinent illustration of Burmese economy of labour coupled with ingenuity. Starting at the bottom of the slope a line of trees is notched lightly on the upper side; proceeding uphill the incision becomes deeper until at the top a line is cut right through; these then fall on their neighbours below, sending the rest down like a pack of cards.

In 1962, Burma lost her place as the world's premier rice exporter. Her population has more than doubled since pre-War days, but lacking the benefits of modern technology her agricultural output has not kept pace. The quality of Burma's rice has also suffered. Farmers have to sell at a fixed price a certain percentage of their crop to the Government for subsequent export. Naturally the free market has been getting the best quality. At present the Government is being advised on modern techniques and new grain varieties by overseas specialists.

'The most calm and contented of mortals' was a 19th-century British view of the Burmese, and this seems true of the great majority of her people today. What possible reason could there be, the Burmese seem to ask, to go about harvesting the abundant fruits of this country with a greater sense of urgency? If they do decide to adopt a less relaxed pace there is little doubt that Burma, with its immense untapped wealth, could become a significant factor in Asia's resource-based economies.

The Peoples of Burma

An ethnographic map of Burma shows a patchwork of peoples. The main group, the Burmans, live in what the British called 'Burma Proper', the lowland areas along the Irrawaddy River. Of today's population of some 35 million, about 23 million are Burmans while the remaining third of the population is divided into six main minority groups and some 60 smaller ones.

There is evidence of man inhabiting the Irrawaddy valley some 5,000 years ago. Perhaps these settlements were staging posts on the main route from Assam to Indochina. But the first permanent settlers of whom we can be certain were the Mons, who had come from the east in about 200 BC. They named the lush country they had discovered Suvannabhumi (Golden Land). Shortly afterwards, first the Pyus and then the Burmans (Mramma) fled their native southeast Tibet in the face of aggression from both the Tibetans and the Chinese. The Pyus formed the spearhead of the migration: they came to rest in the southern reaches of the Irrawaddy while the Burmans themselves settled in central Burma. In the seventh century the Mons, who had settled in the southeast, fought and defeated the Pyus, pushing them north where they apparently merged with the Burmans and made their joint capital at Pagan in 849.

The peoples of these early migrations shared the same Mongoloid features. The Karens, however, are of totally different stock. It is thought that they originated near the Gobi Desert, which their ancestors called the River of Sand. The final major group called the Tai-Shans came south from present-day Yunnan Province in southwest China. During the eighth and ninth centuries they had made periodic raids into Burma, attacking the Pyu Kingdom. When in the 13th century they in turn were conquered by Kublai Khan and became a suzerain state of his empire, a vast exodus of these Tai-Shan people ensued. Many went to Thailand. Another major group of Tai-Shans settled in Upper Burma, building their capitals first at Sagaing and then in 1364 at Ava, and extending their territory as far south as Prome. Thus the situation remained, until the Burmese unified the country (for the second time) in 1555 and the Tai-Shan people, now called Shans, resettled on the high fertile plateau to the east of Ava. In 1752 the ever-turblent Mons, who had been centred on Pegu since its founding in 825, had a final fling against Burmese supremcy; but by 1760 the Burmese had firmly reasserted their power.

At the time of their annexation of Burma, the British felt that 'the great want of the country is population'. A supposed four million lived in Lower Burma and two million in Upper Burma. However, the latter

figure was largely guess-work, since many of the ethnic groups had disappeared into the hills as a result of constant bullying at the hands of the corrupt regime of King Theebaw.

The minority peoples adopted differing attitudes towards their Burman oppressors. The Shans attributed their position to trickery. The two groups were in conflict over a certain tract of land, for which the robust Shans were prepared to fight, but the Burmese called in a hermit to arbitrate, and declared that the winner of the land would be whoever first built a pagoda on the site. In no time the physically superior Shans were in the lead. During the night the crafty Burmese erected a bamboo shell, covered it with cloth and plastered it white. The next morning the Shans were shattered to find the pagoda 'completed' and even with offerings to Buddha in place, so that they never dreamed of looking inside the structure.

The Karens blamed the divine power for their misfortunes. The creator, they believed, threw three clods of earth on the ground: from one sprang the Burmese, from the second the Karens and the third the Kalas (foreigners). Because the Karens were so talkative, the creator threw another handful to the Burmese, thus making them supreme.

These animosities towards the Burmese, deeply ingrained in the culture of many of the minority peoples, help to show that Burma has never been a totally homogeneous nation. Even today, many groups are still fighting for autonomy.

To Sir George Scott, Burmese dress in its rich variety of forms suggested 'wind-stirred tulip beds or a stir about of rainbows.' Of all Burma's ethnic groups the Burmese themselves are the least frivolous dressers. Both men and women wear cotton *longyis* (silk for grand occasions), with neat and often white blouses (*eingyi*) for the women and ordinary cotton shirts for the men. On special occasions, however, Burmese men don white collarless shirts under crisp cotton waist-length jackets. Traditionally both men and women wore their hair long, coiled in a variety of styles on top of their heads, sometimes filled out by a hairpiece. The men would encircle their topknot with a scarf — one finds some older men coiffed thus today — whereas women complete the effect with a bone comb and seasonal flowers. The maidens of Rangoon popularly believed that to sweep the western stairway of the Shwedagon Pagoda was to bring 'the doer beauty of long and black hair in the next existence.'

One of Burma's largest minority groups are the Shans. When, in 1515, they were pushed out of Central Burma, the majority resettled on a high plateau sandwiched between the Kingdoms of Ava and Siam. Fine agriculturalists that they were, the Shans were quick to make the best of its temperate climate and fertile soil. Denied of the independence promised in 1947, they are not allowed to return to their homeland and their activities are closely monitored. Much of the Shan States is still classified as a 'brown area' (and considered unsafe for visitors), as it is controlled by Shan rebels, who have in effect become warlords. The Shan States form a large part of the notorious Golden Triangle which straddles the Burmese—Thai border. It is the growth of opium in this virtually impenetrable region that largely finances the Shan's continuing militant activity.

Of all Burma's ethnic groups only Shan men traditionally wear trousers. With more the appearance of divided skirts, these are baggy garments which hang from a wide loose waist-band folded over and tucked in, and worn with the same crisp jackets as the Burmans. The Shans also originated the rectangular fabric shoulder bag, though today these are carried by men throughout Burma. Shan men and women both use *khamouts* (elegant conical-shaped straw hats similar to those worn in Thailand) as protection against the fierce midday sun.

Three other minority groups living in Shan country are of Mon-Khmer rather than Shan stock: the Padaungs, the Palaungs and the Inthas. The Padaung womenfolk traditionally wore gold rings around their necks and ankles. From the age of six or seven a new ring was added each year. The original purpose of this custom was to repel prospective kidnappers — though one might think these gold-encased 'giraffe women' constituted a positive invitation — but the practice is now illegal for medical reasons. However, ladies of middle age are still to be seen wearing their bondage: once ringed they cannot in effect be released, for the golden corset has stretched and eventually replaced the neck muscles.

The Inthas live near Taunggyi, the capital of the Shan States (founded by Sir George Scott), on the breathtakingly beautiful Inle Lake. Not far away, around Kalaw (a favourite hill station retreat of the colonials, and still a 'little England' of 'stockbroker Tudor' houses surrounded by aster- and snapdragon-filled gardens), are the various Palaung settlements. The Palaung womenfolk are positive birds of paradise against the restful greens of their jungle landscape, and the drab browns of their smoky villages. An unmarried girl might wear a thick red-striped *longyi* with an embroidered green jacket, a cotton tasselled 'halo' perched on her long shiny black hair. Her *longyi* is not tucked in like a Burman's but held in place by a wide white belt. For a working day the velvet jacket is replaced by an embroidered cotton one slightly faded from constant washing and the sun, and the halo discarded in favour of a band around her forehead supporting the weight of a produce-laden basket on her back. When she marries she can substitute a blue or purple jacket with red facing; around her waist hangs a collection of thin lacquer bands and her head is encased by cotton strands from which at the back dangle silver beads — a stunning ensemble worn with great panache. The Palaungs' predominant crop is tea, which they sell 'in the form of hard balls rather larger than cricket balls'; they are also famous for their *lapet* (pickled tea). Before roads reached their remote villages, the *lapet* was carried over the hills to the Irrawaddy where the baskets were strapped to rafts and floated down river semi-submerged.

The other major rebel army, other than the Shans, is that of the Karens. The predominately Christian Karens are excellent soldiers, and during colonial times were widely recruited and promoted within the British Army. Like the Shans, the Karens also felt that they had been unfairly treated as a result of the 1947 Constitution. The Liberation Army, scattered in pockets along Burma's southeastern border with Thailand and in the Irrawaddy delta region, lives on, largely financed by the lucrative smuggling trade.

Both the Kachins, who inhabit the mountainous regions in the north of Burma, and the Chins, whose home is to the west of the country, provided a plentiful source of soldiery for the British. Many Kachins were trained by the American Office of Strategic Services (O.S.S.) during World War II in the fight against the Japanese. The Kachin national dress in particular is another eye-catcher: red calf-length *longyis* worn over tight trousers and black velvet jackets decorated with silver bangles. The men, in their dark *longyis* and blue jackets, carry silver-decorated shoulder bags and elegantly curved silver swords and scabbards.

Geographically, both the Chins and their southerly neighbours, the Arakanese, have been cut off from Burma Proper more than the other minority groups. The Arakanese were able to retain their autonomy over centuries by standing up for themselves — they sacked the Burmese capital on several occasions. The Chins on the other hand were content to keep to their hills. Today, the Burmese remain suspicious of the Arakanese and warn prospective visitors to take care!

Despite the diversity and geographic separation of Burma's ethnic groups, these peoples share with each other and with the Burmans themselves a wide variety of social customs — the *longyi, thanaka* cosmetics, betel and *lapet* are to be found throughout Burma. Pay a call on a Burmese family, whether a friend or total stranger, and you will first be offered tea and then betel and *lapet*. Both delicacies are stored in boxes of either lacquer or silver. In the betel box the top layer will house orange peel, lime and chopped areca nut with fresh betel leaves underneath. Select your leaf, spread it with nuts, lime and peel and chew it, spitting out the strong red juice. The taste is pungent

— said to aid digestion — and leaves the novice a little numb in the mouth and light in the head. *Lapet* is also a mild stimulant but with culinary distinction. Young tea leaves are pressed in bamboo containers and stored in a moist atmostphere which gently ferments them. Before serving, they are mixed with morsels of dried shrimps, roasted peanuts, fried crispy garlic and broad beans.

Another quality which Burma's minority groups share is expertise in weaving. Very often the women of the village will form a weaving guild, each area producing its own distinctive fabric. In more primitive villages it is common to hear the clack of the loom coming from under the house, in the cowshed. The craftswoman sits on the earthern floor, her outstretched legs resting against a bamboo pole, her work suspended from an H-shape frame held taut by a strap around her waist.

The Kachins and Chins, inhabiting the lower-lying and relatively fertile hills in Burma's south and west, have been able to develop settled societies based on a self-sustaining system of slash-and-burn agriculture. Every few years, having exhausted the goodness of the land they have cleared from the jungle, the whole village moves on. Choosing a new site is obviously of critical importance: the traditional method of doing this (and who can be sure it is not practised today?) has a specially Burmese other-worldly quality. Each householder would go out to select a favourite site and from it bring home a clod of earth. That night he places it under his pillow and awaits an auspicious dream. The following day the village soothsayer analyses the dreams. If there is no outright dream winner, a large fowl is cooked and eaten by the householders and the clean bones are put in a earthenware pot. The participants, with eyes averted, each pick out a bone and the one to pick the largest has the honour of leading the village to its new home.

Religion and Society

The Arrival of Buddhism Buddhism is a religious system which acknowledges no supreme deity or god. Gautama Buddha is in fact the fourth Buddha of this 'world cycle' (it is prophesied that the arrival of the fifth Buddha will bring to an end the current world cycle). Many believe Gautama Buddha was born Prince Siddhartha of the Gautama clan in India in around 566 BC, although the records vary on this date. At the age of 30 he left his home, wife and son to become a holy man and for six years he led a life of austerity (eating, the legend has it, one grain of rice a day). Eventually he realized this was not the way to salvation, so he began to advocate and teach the path of the 'Middle Way'. Put most simply, this is the avoidance of extremes, the cultivation of tranquillity, the acceptance of *karma*. The goal of all Buddhists is to attain Nirvana, freedom from the endless cycle of rebirths. The realization of this goal is in the hands of the individual. A higher state in future incarnations can only be achieved by living a pious life, adhering to the Five Precepts (the Buddhist Commandments), and following the Middle Way.

Buddhism came to Burma in several stages. Around the beginning of the Christian era Indian merchants and missionaries travelled to Burma, teaching both the Northern and Southern Buddhist scriptures. The great Indian King Ashoka, promoter of Buddhism, is said to have visited the Shwedagon Pagoda in around 260 BC to pay homage to its relics of the four Buddhas. If this was indeed the case, Ashoka's endorsement would have added considerably to the momentum of Buddhism in Burma. But it was not until 1056 that Sri Lankan Theravada Buddhism was fully established in Burma by King Anawrahta. The Burmese had always cherished the concept that all men and women are equal. To find these very concepts at the heart of Buddhism, the religion which was being sponsored by their king, made it readily acceptable. The Buddhism adopted in Burma was the Southern or Theravada (Hinayana) denomination.

The *Nat* Spirit Gods Burma's brand of Theravada Buddhism is unique. When King Anawrahta was converted to Theravada Buddhism in late 1056, he realized that he was not going to be able to stamp out entirely the intricate web of animism, alchemy and tantric rites practised by the Ari monks and their followers. So he disbanded the elements he regarded as most irreverent and then showed his tolerence of the *nats* (spirit gods) by allowing them into the pagoda precinct. Anawrahta decreed that Thagyamin, the King of the Gods and guardian of Buddhism, was to be added to the original 36 *nats* and considered their leader. Images of the 37, in attitudes of worship, were

then placed in the newly-built Shwezigon Pagoda in Pagan (not to be confused with the Shwedagon Pagoda in Rangoon), in order that 'the people come to worship their old gods, and then they will discover the truth of the new faith of Buddhism.'

Today there are still 37 'inner *nats*' (those allowed into the pagoda precinct), and hundreds of 'outer *nats*'. The list of 37 has varied somewhat from Anawrahta's time, and is made up of a strange mélange of heroes and tragic historical characters, the majority of whom met violent ends. The exception was Kunshaw, 'The Lord of the White Umbrella' and father of Anawrahta. Kunshaw's father was killed before he was born and the throne usurped. His mother fled the court, bringing up her son in poverty. On the death of the usurper's son, Kunhsaw was proclaimed king by popular demand and, out of the goodness of his heart, took into his palace the two pregnant wives of his predecessor and made them his queens. Their sons he brought up as his own. However, on reaching adulthood, his ungrateful stepsons persuaded Kunshaw to enter a monastery and then deposed him. Years later, when Anawrahta regained the throne and offered it to his elderly father, Kunshaw refused: 'I am old to look upon, old in years. Be now king thyself,' he protested. He died shortly afterwards and was elevated to the 'nathood', but as a monk, not a king.

Nats play an important role in the everyday life of a Burman; if not properly appeased they can prove very troublesome. The beauty of a Burmese maiden is enhanced by adorning her hair with a sprig of blossom; likewise fresh flowers decorate tastefully laid stalls in the market. These are not, as one might imagine, efforts to glamorize the 'shop window' but are in fact signs of homage to the *nats*. You will see the outer *nats* shrines everywhere, perched in trees or housed in little bamboo hutches along the wayside. The most evident of these are the shrines of the 'house *nat*'. On the south side of nearly every house hangs a coconut. The strips of red and yellow fabric with which these are sometimes adorned are offerings to Eing Saung, the protector of the household. In times gone by the four corner posts of the house, which were thought to be his favourite abode, were draped in white cloth.

The traditional home of the *nats* is Mount Popa, which sits in the middle of the arid Myingyan plain southeast of Pagan.

Nat culture remained deeply ingrained in both secular and religious matters. Included in the court oath of loyalty to the Burmese kings (read before an image of Buddha) was the statement that by serving his royal master with obedience, the candidate 'under the aid of the 5,000 *nats* that guard religion' would be free from all 96 diseases. It was only with the building of Mandalay in 1857 that a particularly barbaric *nat* custom was brought to an end. Previously, during the construction of a new city, someone would be buried alive under each corner of the perimeter wall. These unfortunates were supposed then to be reincarnated as evil *nats* and to keep at bay the city's foes.

Not all *nats* are of such violent disposition. 'The little lady of the flute' acts as guardian and playmate of children (when engaged in the latter role causing them to smile in their sleep). Happily, *nat* worship today manifests this gentler side of its nature, with daily offerings to one's favourite spirit to bring safety and success in one's everyday life.

The Burmese Cosmos Also apart from the main stream of Theravada Buddhism is the Burmese concept of the cosmos. In the centre stands mythical Mount Meru, shaped like half a serrated eggshell upside down, half above an ocean and half below. On its slopes are the six seats of Devas, the beings who by good works and incessant meditation 'have risen above man's estate on the path to Nirvana'. Above them are the 16 seats of Brahmas — those who live in sublime contemplation. Below are the eight great hells, and the numerous smaller ones. Round Mount Meru extends the vast Thamohodaya Ocean containing thousands of small islands clustered around four main ones: North, South, East and West. The human race inhabits the southern island, the Burmese, Chinese and the Indians on the main island itself, the rest on its satellites. Whereas life on the southern island is difficult, on the remainder paradise reigns, especially on the northern island, where 'gorgeous clothes hang ready-made from the trees, dainty meals of all kinds grow up and cook themselves.' But the inhabitants are unhappy for they are always reborn on the same island thus making it impossible to progress towards Nirvana. The 24 Buddhas from the 64 previous worlds and the four Buddhas of the present era of existence all reached Nirvana via the southern island.

Quest for Nirvana 'How great a favour has the Lord Buddha bestowed on me in manifesting to me his law through the observation of which I may escape hell and secure my salvation.' To the Buddhist Burman the quest for Nirvana — literally the extinction of all passions and desires, which has also come to mean a state of beatitude — is the pivot of life. Nirvana is the zenith of the Ladder of Existence, the Four States of Punishment being its nadir. An individual's position on the Ladder will depend on how much merit has been accrued during his previous lives. Those unfortunates doomed to the States of Punishment have to endure thousands of years in bubbling furnaces, their ever-renewing flesh being torn to shreds by odious gargoyles and five-headed dogs. The destiny of mortals who did not curb their passions and were abusive on earth is the profoundest state of hell, the 'Bong of Animals'. Some animals, though, such as the hare, white

elephant and pigeon, are exempt from the Bong, as they are believed
to have been former incarnations of Gautama Buddha. The vulture,
too, is above the Bong as it does not take life but rather lives off
carrion. Once having fallen into these macabre states of hell it is not
clear how the victim climbs out; but avoiding them appears to depend
on close adherence to the Five Great Precepts, while one's advance up
the Ladder is a question of accruing merit.

A further dimension to this accounting system is *karma*. If one's
former life has been meritorious, one is reborn not only higher up the
scale but with good *karma*. There is no recognised method of
improving one's *karma*, though some employ a *bedin-saya*, a sort of
fortune-teller, to prescribe a *khame* or charm to keep evil influences at
bay.

The collection of merit is therefore all important, as it can save a
soul from the bubbling Bong of Animals and store credit for a future
life. If one stops in a village, hot and weary from a long motor-car
journey, the villagers will provide *lapet* or their local brew (such as
toddy wine), hose down the tyres, offer to show one their pagoda and
suggest a siesta on the cool floor of one of their houses. These gestures
of hospitality are offered with such charm that the traveller is
unconscious of the underlying ulterior motive — to gain merit. This
search for merit is evident in practically every aspect of Burmese daily
life. At one end of the scale is the placing by the roadside of clay pots
from which any thirsty traveller may refresh himself. At the other end
is pagoda building: 'No work of merit is so richly paid as the building
of a pagoda.' (Conversely, and, one is inclined to feel, somewhat
unfairly, the repairing of an existing pagoda, unless it happens to be
one of the renowned shrines such as the Shwedagon, gains no merit for
the repairer, but only for the original donor.) This is surely one of the
key factors underlying the astonishing profusion of pagodas with which
the Burmese countryside, and in particular the plains of the Irrawaddy,
are so liberally sprinkled. Of course it is only the rich who are able to
make this grand gesture. For the majority, the quest for Nirvana
consists of attempting to live by the Five Great Precepts, preparing
food for the monks and indulgence in premeditated acts of merit such
as freeing caged birds. (One might well inquire how the catching of the
birds in the first place affected the merit of those concerned!) There is
even a festival for the liberation of fish. In the rainy season when the
rivers rise to form flood lakes, the trapped fish are caught and kept in
huge 'chatties'. They are later released amid much fun and frolic into
the river.

Becoming a Monk Until the age of 12, when the male child
normally has his *shin-pyu* ('to make a monk'), his Buddhistic life

cannot commence and he is cast among the animals on the Ladder of
Existence. The day he is accepted as an *upathaka* — a believer — it
becomes within his power to raise or lower his status in his next life.
The *shin-pyu* is an occasion of feasting. An auspicious day is chosen by
the astrologer, invitations are dispensed by the female members of the
family, not in the form of cards but in packets of *lapet*. As the day
draws near, the novice receives instruction in monastic etiquette. In
some rural districts the boy is confined to his house for seven days
before his initiation for fear that jealous evil spirits will kidnap him.
On the appointed day he is dressed in princely garments and jewels,
mounted on a white pony and leads a gay procession around the
village. This journey symbolizes Prince Siddhartha's royal life, which
he renounced in order to search for enlightenment. The journey
ended, the boy disrobes before the head of the monastery, has his
head shaved and is washed by rubbing with seeds and saffron. Then,
prostrating himself before the head monk, he asks in Pali for
admittance to the monastery so that he may strive towards gaining
Nirvana. Once accepted he is given his monastic robes, a begging bowl
is hung around his neck and, while festivities continue in his house,
follows the monk to his new home. Buddhism abhors physical suffering
and a small boy's life in a monastery is not a hard one. He will learn
and observe the ten precepts (the five most important, The Five Great
Precepts, forbid taking life, stealing, adultery, lying and drinking
intoxicating liquor), learn his lessons, beg for his food and carry out
domestic duties in the monastery. Depending on how pious his family
is his stay could be anything from one week to several months (or
indeed for life).

Monks and Burmese Society Supporting Burma's substantial
monastic population imposes heavy demands on the country's
economy, but society expects nothing in return save the merit gained
through guardianship of the monks. However, the situation was
different prior to Burma's annexation by the British Empire, when the
country's education was in the hands of the monks. All boys attended
the monastic school free of charge where they learned the Buddhist
scriptures and the rudiments of mathematics as well as how to read and
write. In those days Burma could boast the highest rate of literacy in
Asia. The British started to modify this system in the 19th century by
introducing lay and missionary schools. But it was not until after
independence that radical changes occurred. When the Ne Win
government came to power in the 1960s the Buddhist establishment
was considered potential political opposition. To neutralize the support
that Ne Win felt was being given to the ethnic rebels, he commanded
all monks to be registered, exposed those living openly with women

'under my nose' in Rangoon, and removed the education system from monastic control. Today, education is run by the State and only in the remotest areas are monastic schools still to be found.

Although deprived of a practical role in society, the ubiquitous monks continue to exert a profound influence by their example (though the record, like that of all religious orders the world has ever known, is by no means unblemished), and, perhaps more important, by serving as a constant reminder of the way of the Buddha. This is reflected in the reverence and piety in which they are held by the vast majority of the lay population. So far as the monks themselves are concerned their life is certainly austere, though by no means unpleasant. The calm of monastic routine, uncluttered by material paraphernalia, provides the ideal environment in which to study and adopt the teachings of the Middle Way — a life of no extremes in which every thought, word and deed should contribute towards reaching Nirvana.

The Status of Burmese Women The culture and social structure of Burma are intertwined with Buddhism. Burma boasts a natural democracy and liberation for its womenfolk. From the lowliest origins they could spin to the top; the last queen, Supayalat, was the granddaughter of a fisherman. There has never been any caste system or primogeniture (absence of the latter of course fuelling innumerable palace intrigues and murders). Burmese women have for centuries enjoyed the freedom and equality only recently hankered after by their Western sisters — able to choose their own marriage partner, to remain the owner of any money brought to the union and with freedom of divorce. A Burmese marriage is only a public declaration between the couple involved that they wish to be man and wife. This emphasis on the individual helps to explain why there is no such thing as a family name in Burma. Nor, therefore, do women change their names on marriage. During the days of the monarchy the Burmese did not support a middle class; as Dr Htin Aung says, 'not because as in Czarist Russia there were only aristocrats and serfs, but simply because there was neither an upper nor a lower class.' As land was considered a gift of nature and could be acquired by clearing it there was no landed gentry, the village was the basic unit of society, and was generally self-sufficient and self-maintained. Within that unit the women played their equal part. It was not (and is not today) uncommon for the women to be the business managers while the men cared for the children.

Festivals and Theatre 'It is the nature of the Burmese to make festivals' — an assertion amply borne out by the Burmese addiction to festivals and theatre. Like practically every important aspect of

Burmese society, and in particular those involving entertainment, they take place under the auspices of the pagoda.

Burma's rainy season, during which merrymaking is impractical, coincides with the Buddhist 'Lent', which marks the period of Buddha's meditation prior to his enlightenment. They both end in October. From then until the following July every town and village will periodically buzz with one or another festival of some description. There are national festivals for celebrating the New Year (the Water Festival), the harvest, the end of Buddhist Lent (the Festival of Light), the presentation of new robes to the monks (the Weaving Festival) and many more. Then, also, each pagoda will have its own birthday festival and each community its favourite *nat* to honour. In addition special events, such as the raising of a new *hti* (umbrella) for a pagoda, will require an individual celebration.

Days before a festival, a village of bamboo stalls mushrooms around the pagoda. Men, women and children dash about arranging their wares; sideshows of old-fashioned roundadouts with brightly-coloured papier-mâché animals materialize. A carefree carnival spirit permeates the air. If the festival is at one of the more renowned pagodas, pilgrims — including whole families with goods and chattels stuffed into bullock and pony carts — converge from far and wide.

The frenzied preparations give way to the commencement of the festival itself. As the dawn mist hovers over the festival ground the pagoda wakes. The swish of brooms can be heard as devotees sweep away the remnants of yesterday's offerings. The arrival at the flower stall of the day's fresh produce brings a heady aroma of jasmine and rosebuds and awakens the men and women whose job it is to wire the blooms into nosegays. Fires are kindled; some people prepare their own breakfast, others hunt out the *mohingha* stalls which have sprung up as if by magic. The *mohingha* vendor sits behind a low table covered with a multitude of bowls. These contain an eccentric-seeming variety of delicacies — chopped coriander, fried garlic, bean crackers, hard-boiled eggs, fish sausage, sesame nuts. On one side is a large basin of rice noodles, with a muslin cloth to keep the heat in and the flies out; on the other a large cauldron of fish soup steams over a charcoal fire. Hands flickering, the vendor combines in an empty bowl, a handful of noodles, a sprinkling of each of the chopped ingredients (deftly cutting the eggs and fish sausages with scissors), a ladleful of fish broth, a pinch of chili powder and finally a squeeze of fresh lime: delicious! A popular and expert *mohingha* cook can serve 250 bowls single-handed at one breakfast session.

A festival may last for up to a week. During the daytime there will

be bands, processions to the pagoda, dancing — an extravaganza of colours, movement and noise, especially noise — generally incorporating the particular activity which symbolizes the purpose of the festival. However, the peak of many festivals occurs at night. At the end of Buddhist Lent, for example, the return of Buddha to earth is marked by lights on every conceivable building; while during the Weaving Festival, young girls compete by the light of the full moon in making new robes for the monks.

Festival evenings and nights are frequently devoted to *pwes*. According to Sir George Scott, 'There is no nation on the face of the earth so fond of theatrical representations as the Burmese.' As light begins to fade, activity centres on the large stage. The auditorium is a fenced-in area with rush matting on the ground and is free to all, so it's first-come-first-served. The whole family settles down for the night's entertainment with bedrolls for the children and tiffin boxes. For the less provident, hawkers weave in and out selling nuts, nibbles, cigars and cigarettes. The Burmese are a nation of smokers from nearly the smallest ('Burmese children never smoke before they can walk.') to the oldest grandmother who sits, intent on the *pwe*, an enormous cigar clenched between her gums and holding a small basin to catch the ash and sparks — for Burmese cigars sometimes behave akin to fireworks. If more substantial sustenance is required, a galaxy of food stalls with such delights as 'husband and wife' onion cakes (cooked in separate moulds and then joined) is stationed around the fence. A Burmese theatre audience resembles nothing so much as a restless, constantly murmuring sea.

There are two distinct groups of *pwe*: light and serious drama. The first is of the variety-show genre. Burmese, like Chinese, is a monosyllabic language and affords ample opportunity for puns. However, the highly developed Burmese art of clowning with all the facial subleties of mime, lets even the non-Burmese in on most of the humour. The second group consists of the more serious Wethandaya Wutha (the Ten Great Birth Stories), which illustrate the last ten incarnations of Buddha before he attained enlightenment.

Both types of theatre involve song, dance and dramatic music, and the cast is supported by an eight- to ten-man orchestra. The most spectacular instruments are the *saing-waing* and the *kyi-waing*. Both are made of elaborately carved (and often gilded) panels standing 0.6 to 0.9 metres (two to three feet) high and forming a circle some 1.5 metres (five feet) in diameter. Suspended from the inside of the panels are either drums or gongs with the player sitting in the middle. He constantly tunes his drums by applying and kneading a sticky paste of burnt rice husk. There are no written scores, so all the music must be learnt by ear. Each group has an apprentice who plays the *wa le'kot* (bamboo cymbals): the apprenticeship system ensures the music's passage from one generation to the next. This strange orchestra can produce effects ranging from the ponderous and lovelorn to the warlike and triumphant, playing for hours on end with unflagging zeal. The Western ear takes time to adjust to its discordant crashes and rhythmic eccentricities, but in time they cast a mesmeric spell. The dancers also display tremendous stamina. Of the 120 basic steps most are executed with bent knees. Lissom bodies, clad in court dress from the Ava period, perform a series of sinuous, tentacular movements. The skirt is a narrow sequined tube with the added hazard of a 0.6-metre (two-foot) train which the dancer, with consummate skill and elegance, flicks out of the way with a supple foot, without disturbing the smooth glide of the dance. The steps for men and women are the same and to see a man dancing the role of a princess is by no means unusual.

In early April Burmans seemingly go mad: battalions of young people line the streets armed with vats of water, from which they fill all available receptacles in order to throw the contents at hapless passers-by. Only the elderly and the monks are exempt. Sir George Scott recounts the following experience of a newly arrived Englishman. 'The victim reached Rangoon on the second day of the water-feast, and having no Indian outfit got himself up in a tall hat, frockcoat, and the rest. . . . On the verandah he found three or four Burmese girls, who forthwith asked permission to throw water on him. He naturally supposed they were asking whether he wanted to see the master of the house, and nodded violently. Whereupon they capsized their bowls of water over him, including the hat in the libation. The astonished man took it to be the custom of the country to cool down over-heated foreigners, but thought the inclusion of his hat an unnecessary detail.' This three-day orgy of water throwing marks the beginning of the New Year and the visit to earth of Thagyamin, the King of the *Nats*. The festivities start with an *a-kyo-nay* ('preparing to greet day'), when sacred water pots are filled and made fragrant by the addition of aromatic leaves. Food is prepared both for the monasteries and the neighbours, and bamboo stands are erected for communal hair-washing. The noblest part of the body must be clean to honour the celestial guest. In the days of the monarchy there was a ceremonial washing (*tha-gyan daw gyi*) of the king's hair. The water for this ceremony was carried from the springs of the beautiful Gaung Se Kyun (Head-Washing Island). This islet, near Moulmein, seemingly hangs above the water, inspiring the idea that it was suspended from the heavens by an invisible thread. The hair-washing takes place at dusk in readiness for the god's arrival at midnight. A special shampoo is used, made by soaking the dried bark of the *tha-yaw* tree, then boiling and pounding acacia seeds, then mixing the acacia powder with *tha-yaw* water.

The god's arrival is heralded by a gunfire salute. The large pots are filled with water, and sacred *tha-byay* leaves are ceremoniously emptied, after which the water throwing revel begins. Children armed with water pistols ambush the unsuspecting, young maidens exchange their thin muslin blouses for ones of thicker fabric to avoid any immodesty when their garments become wet and clinging. During the next three days everyone tries to live according to the Five Great Precepts (the Buddhist code of behaviour) and children are especially well-behaved. Thagyamin, they are warned, brings with him two books, one bound in dog-skin to record the names of those who are sinful, the other bound in gold for those who have gained merit. The *a-tetnay* ('rising day') marks Thagyamins's return to the heavens and ends the festivities, though some enthusiastic revellers squeeze in another day, declaring that he has returned to earth to collect his forgotten pipe or umbrella.

Burmese Food

Burmese cuisine can be delicious: *mohingha*, the traditional breakfast, *ohn no khaukswe* and *lapet* rank with some of Asia's best dishes. For a short-term visitor to Burma, however, it can be difficult to sample the real thing. Most restaurants serve Chinese food and the hotels British Raj-style curries.

The Burmese take their food seriously. Daw Mi Mi Khaing explains, 'Burmese food is for eating mainly just before morning's pleasantness is lost to the heat of noon, and again as the cool of evening falls. Ideally, you should, minutes before eating, have a quick pouring bath, put on clean clothes, and go straight to table.' A breakfast of *mohingha* is a pleasure indeed; a gentle aroma of banana stem and lemon grass rises from a bowl of steaming fish soup and rice noodles, topped by coriander leaf, fried garlic, chilli powder, fried corn crackers and a squeeze of lime, washed down with Burmese tea. *Ohn no khaukswe*, the other 'national' dish, is again a noodle and soup affair — in Western terminology it might be termed a casserole, for there are chicken chunks in the soup. This time the noodles are of wheat, and the soup is strongly flavoured with coconut.

The pickled tea leaf the Burmese call *'lapet'* is eaten at all times of day, perhaps as the finale to a rich dinner or when visitors arrive unexpectedly. On such occasions a drink of tea and the lacquer box containing *lapet* will be produced. Inside the box are different compartments filled with *lapet*, fried garlic, toasted sesame seeds, fried broad bean seeds and salt. *Lapet* is bought ready-prepared in the market, then kneaded with a little sesame oil at home. It should be eaten thus: 'Take a pinch of each of two or three things together with *lapet*, between tips of three fingers only. In between, wipe fingers and sip tea. Wash fingers only at the end. This is the connoisseur's way.' The taste is refreshing and good, though quite sharp. Those who like spinach salad will be immediate converts.

With Burma's abundant supply of fruit and vegetables, salad is served with each meal. Seasonal ingredients are tossed in sesame oil, with crispy nuts and coriander added. In spring it is *marian* (*mayan thi*) season. This is a small green and mauve fruit which resembles an unripe walnut. Its piquant flavour in a salad is a winner.

Of all the dishes the Western palate will sample, the Burmese speciality least likely to appeal is *ngapi*. 'The smell of *ngapi*,' remarked the by-no-means over-sensitive Sir George Scott, 'is certainly not charming to an uneducated nose.' *Ngapi* is a relish which can accompany any dish. There are three distinct types: *'ngapi gaung*,' consisting of whole fish pressed, dried and later eaten baked; *'ngapi seinsa*,' made from the squeezed and fermented juices of shrimp, which is stored in earthenware pots, not dissimilar to anchovy paste; and third and most pungent, '*ngapi yecho*' (*taungtha*). This is made from small fish which are left uncleaned in the sun for a day or two ('by which time their condition is better imagined than closely investigated'); then they are salted, pounded and stored in clay pots.

If you are interested in sampling Burmese fare, ask your hotel or guesthouse for local specialities or, even better, try some of the street restaurants. Festivals always provide a good hunting ground for *mohingha*. A few sensible precautions are necessary: make sure the food is cooked freshly or is steaming hot; wash the spoon, fork and cup with the hot tea provided (you will see the locals do it); *never* drink tap water and *never* have a drink with ice in it or eat a piece of already cut fruit or vegetable. Follow these tips and adventurous eating in Burma can be a source of true serendipity.

Shopping in Burma

Shopping in Burma offers many rewards but it also can be a frustrating experience. Normally a tourist's first foray in search of souvenirs, objects d'arts, or antiques and other more substantial items will lead them to Rangoon's Bogyoke Market located on Bogyoke Road. There they will find an amazing collection of fascinating items: finely crafted mother of pearl; beautiful silks, lacquerware products of every description; bizarre nick-nacks dating from colonial times (some of which may be of considerable value to collectors back home); cigars; gold and silver jewellery; jade bracelets and many other interesting items. However, when one calculates a desired purchase price (always calculated in burmese *kyats*), one will probably discover that its cost can vary from very cheap to outrageously high, depending if the vendor figures the cost at the black market currency rate or the official bank rate. Furthermore, many of the most desirable items like antiques or large lacquerware pieces, such as chests and screens, *may not* be taken or shipped out of the country (contrary, of course, to the merchant's assurances) without obtaining proper documentation — a process so complex and time consuming that it is virtually impossible to accomplish on a one-week tourist visa. Thorough searches at the airport upon departure are very common. Nevertheless, there are plenty of interesting products that make lovely (and legal) souvenirs. In Rangoon, one of the best values are tailor-made shirts and dresses; buy the material in St John's Market, which deals in black market goods, and take them to any tailor downtown with your size requirements.

Lacquerware

Pagan is the centre of Burma's lacquer industry and has been producing fine lacquerware since the time of King Anawrahta. It is not clear whether the king imported the craft from Nanzhao, which he visited in an attempt to acquire Buddha's tooth, or whether it was brought north from Pegu by the conquered Mon artisans whom he re-settled in Pagan. The majority of these lacquer articles are for domestic use, such as betel boxes, cosmetics boxes, and drinking cups. Raw black lacquer is tapped from the *thitsi* tree, a variety of sumac, which comes in the main from northern Burma and the Shan States. Traditionally the frame is woven in bamboo wickerwork or a horse-hair mix, though today wooden bases are used for many articles such as trays and cigarette boxes, as this makes them cheaper to produce and more durable. On the wicker base a coat of lacquer is applied and left to dry in a cool, airy place — the sun produces blisters — for several days. After a couple of days, when the lacquer is quite hard, it is evenly covered with a paste called *thayo*. Depending on the quality of the article, *thayo* is made from finely-

Upon your return from upcountry several days later, you will find a well tailored garment and a bill that is almost embarrassingly cheap (a man's shirt, for instance, can cost as little as US$3 including material). Other exceptional values (even at legal exchange rates) include mother-of-pearl products, silver jewellery and, strangely enough, Stoloichnaya vodka available in duty-free shops for only US$5 or US$6! Don't miss the second-hand bookshops in Rangoon.

Elsewhere in Burma, Pagan is the best place to buy lacquerware products; Mandalay is where the intricately woven and lavishly adorned tapestries known as 'Kalagas' are produced; and the hill station of Maymyo has some of the most interesting 'antique' objects available. To get an idea of the range of handicrafts produced in Burma, it is worth visiting the official exports showroom known as the Myanma Export-Import Co-operative Syndicate, located in Rangoon at 185–7 Pansodan Street.

Despite the difficulties in trying to 'export' Burmese products, the determined treasure hunter is more likely to find an extraordinary object tucked away in the corner of a shop in Burma than anywhere else in Southeast Asia.

ground bone ash and paddy husk, burnt and strained through a cloth, or, for articles for everyday use, clay and peanut husk. When this coating has dried, the lacquer item is put on a hand lathe and polished, using ash or a bamboo strip. This whole process is repeated several times. Then the foreground colour is added. On the cheaper pieces the decorations (traditional designs predominate) are simply painted on; the more expensive ones are engraved with a tool called a *kauk*. Normally, three colours are used, each colour representing several layers and a great deal of time and effort.

Raw lacquer has a variety of other uses. When spread over marble or clay it enables gold leaf to stick (part of the early morning ablutions of the Mahamuni Image in Mandalay is to coat the Buddha with a thin film of lacquer) (see page 119). It is also used to waterproof boats and sometimes umbrellas. There are several lacquer trade schools in Pagan and the main street is filled with lacquer shops. One can just go in to the back of the shops to watch master craftsmen and their apprentices busily applying these time-honoured methods.

Vessel and cover on stand in the shape of a karaweik *(sacred bird). Gold, chased and decorated with filigree work, and inlaid with rubies and imitation emeralds. Burmese; 19th century.*

Rangoon

Burma's capital city, the home of 3.5 million people, is a city of style and dilapidated grandeur. For as long as they survive, the broad, leafy boulevards and slightly pompous architecture will recall the serene confidence of the British Raj of the mid-19th century.

Strolling through Rangoon is both agreeable and safe — the main hazard being yawning holes in the pavements. However, unlike Noel Coward's mad dogs and Englishmen, you should avoid wandering around during the noon hours as it can be extremely hot.

Rangoon bustles — if bustle is the word — gently. One rarely sees anyone pick up their *longyi* and run for a bus: there is always another one not far behind. In recent years Rangoon's traffic has taken on a different look, and there is now a noticeable percentage of new Japanese trucks alongside the 1950s Buicks. This is because every Burmese sailor abroad is allowed to import one vehicle a year which he then sells off. The 'Kobe Irrawaddy Trading Company Limited' in Japan deals exclusively with converting vehicles for this market. 'The young women always used to want to marry a professional man, now a girl's greatest wish is to marry a seaman', is a familiar lament.

Little markets and food stalls are everywhere. At a busy intersection a man with a bird-cage squats under a large tree. People stop to buy a bird and, instead of taking it home, let it free in order to gain some merit. Around another corner sits the proprietor of a thriving typing business tapping away at an ancient upright machine. There are marvellous bookshops, antique and curio shops to browse in and, for those interested in old photographs, the plates of one P Klier, Rangoon's society photographer of the turn of the century, are held by a shop which will make up prints if you wish.

Rangoon is built on a spit of land surrounded on three sides by water. On the west and south by the Hlaing or Rangoon River, which flows out of the Irrawaddy and, 32 kilometres (20 miles) south of the city, into the Bay of Bengal to the east of the main Irrawaddy delta. On the east side of the city is the Pazunduang Creek.

History of Rangoon

Rangoon's history is firmly linked to that of the Shwedagon Pagoda, one of Asia's pre-eminent religious monuments. For well over 2,000 years a community has been in existence around Singuttara Hill on which the pagoda stands, both to accommodate visiting pilgrims and attend to the maintenance and the other needs of the great building. For most of its history it was part of one or another of the Mon

Kingdoms, and at one time served as the residence of the Regent of Pegu. It also acted as the guard station to the entrance of the Irrawaddy, the rest of the delta being virtually unnavigable. However, without doubt, its primary *raison d'être* has always been religious. A merchant by the name of Gaspar Balbi visited Dagon, as it was then called, in 1586 and was much impressed by its profusion of monasteries: 'Wooden houses gilded and adorned with delicate gardens after their custome wherein their talapoing, which are their friars, dwell and look to the pagoda or varella of Dagon.'

The Burmans, led by King Alaungpaya, finally conquered the city in 1753. It was he who founded the Third Burmese Empire and gave Rangoon its modern name, which means 'end of strife' or 'city of peace'. At the end of the second Anglo-Burmese war in 1852, Rangoon came into the hands of the British. By this time it was 'no better than a village with the Governor's house and stockade in the middle of it.' The stockade was taken down, the surrounding marshes drained and a fine city, laid out on a grid system, complete with all the colonial trappings, was constructed. During World War II Rangoon was occupied by the Japanese but luckily escaped serious bomb damage. So today's city is much as the British left it. Indeed, most buildings haven't had a new coat of paint since 1939.

Sights in Rangoon

The Shwedagon Pagoda

The Shwedagon shimmers above the city of Rangoon — pure beauty, magically blended with an aura of legend and history. At the end of the previous world five lotus buds sprang up on Singuttara Hill (where the pagoda stands today); from each of these plants rose a sacred bird carrying a sacred yellow robe. These robes symbolized the coming of the five Buddhas who would guide the next world towards Nirvana. As foretold, four of the Buddhas have appeared in the present world. (The fifth, Maitreya, is still awaited; his coming is expected to mark the end of the current world cycle.) Each of the four has left a relic to be enshrined on Singuttara Hill: Kakusandha, his staff; Konagamana, his water filter; Kassapa, a piece of his robe; and Gautama, eight hairs. On the seventh day following the enlightenment of Gautama Buddha, two Burmese merchant brothers, Taphussa and Bhallika, were travelling with a caravan of 500 carts when, for no apparent reason, the oxen stopped 'as if chained to the earth'. Thereupon a *nat*, who had seen the merchants' mother in a previous existence, appeared before them with the news of the Buddha's enlightenment. The brothers arrived to pay homage to the Buddha, bearing 'rice cakes and honey food'. In

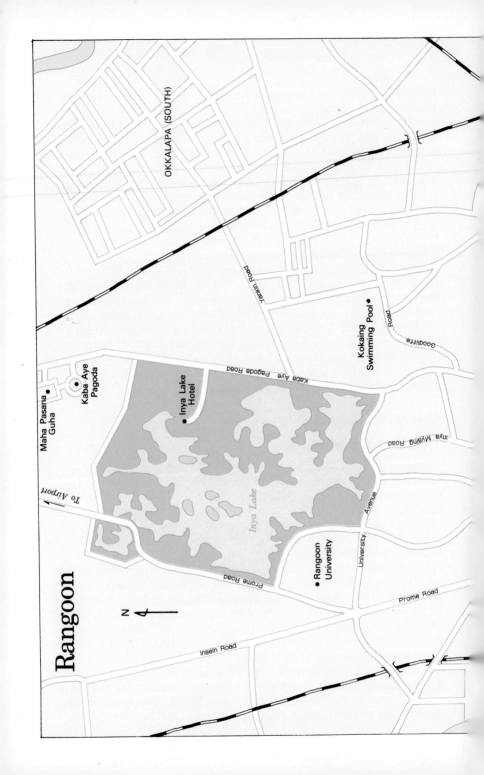

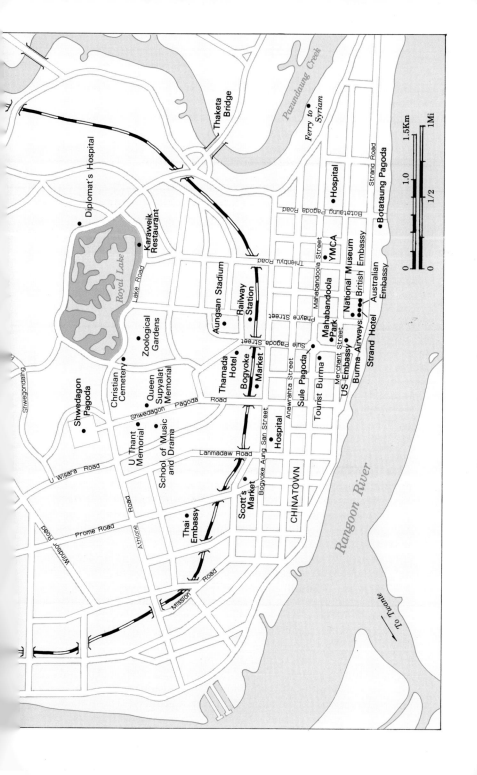

return for their allegiance the Buddha plucked eight hairs from his head and bade the brothers return to their country and enshrine them on Singuttara Hill along with the previous Buddha's relics. After a long and arduous journey they arrived in Burma and enlisted the help of Sakka, the King of the *Nats*, to locate Singuttara Hill. Eventually, it and the other relics were discovered and all the treasures enshrined together.

Thereafter, the pagoda's history emerges from the legendary into half light and eventually, recorded history. The first notable pilgrim to the hill was Ashoka, the great Indian emperor, purveyor of Theravada Buddhism and convenor of the Third Buddhist Synod. He came to pay homage to the relics in about 260 BC. The jungle had enveloped the pagoda, and Ashoka ordered it to be cleared and restored. Succcessive kings continued to maintain and enlarge the pagoda. The most extensive alterations were carried out during the 15th century when Queen Viharadevi (or Sin Saw Bu) had the stupa raised to the height of 95 metres (302 feet) and, for the first time, gilded. Over the years the Shwedagon's development continued and more and more accessories were added (and occasionaly removed). In 1612 Felipe de Brito, the Portuguese adventurer who governed the port of Syriam for 13 years, made off with a bronze and brass bell weighing 18,000 *viss* (almost 32 tons), intending to re-cast it into cannon. But 'in the power of the Buddha' the boat bearing it to Syriam sank in the Rangoon River. (The following year Syriam was sacked by the Burmese king, and de Brito taken prisoner and impaled.)

This pagoda has suffered both the ravages of war and natural disasters. In 1768, six years of restoration were necessary following an earthquake which devastated the top portion. The present form of the pagoda is the result of this work. King Hsinbyusin had his craftsmen encase the exquisite lotus leaves and banana bud at the stupa's summit in solid gold — 3,538 gold and silver tiles, ten million bricks and 100,000 brass screws were used.

Fifty years later on 11 May 1824, British troops sailed up the river to land, unchallenged, in Rangoon and immediately made the 'Great Pagoda' their key position. 'Considered as military posts,' noted T A Trant, a British staff officer, 'the Dagon was of utmost importance, its elevated brick terraces, which obviated the necessity of additional fortifications, and its commanding situation, rendering it the key of our whole position.' This occupation was short-lived, but a little less than 30 years later, the British returned in force. In April 1852, a flotilla of 15 warships and 15 steamers (under the command of Rear Admiral Charles Austen, brother of the novelist Jane Austen) sailed into Rangoon carrying 6,000 men and 35 pieces of artillery. This time the

British troops had to fight to gain control of the strategic pagoda. They were to remain in occupation for the next 77 years.

Shamefully, the temptation of their surroundings proved impossible to resist. 'There is a sailor busy with his pickaxe,' observed W F B Laurie, a historian of the second Burmese war, 'excavating a huge golden image with as much coolness as if he were digging a trench. He is looking for treasure.' One officer ordered a passage to be dug into the bowels of the Shwedagon. Under questioning, he claimed that the purpose was to ascertain whether it could be used as a gunpowder magazine. Perhaps the most serious act of vandalism against the Great Pagoda was the attempted removal of the Singu Min Bell. However, this project met a similar fate to that of de Brito's earlier plundering. The raft on which it was being transported to a waiting ship capsized and the attempt was abandoned. Later, the people of Rangoon salvaged the bell and reinstated it in the pagoda.

The Shwedagon is 'calm and sublime, with the smiling look as is seen on the face of Buddha, not smiling in the eyes or mouth, but in the serene expression of inward calm.' Considering the Great Pagoda's haphazard evolution, this totality of impact on the spirit as well as on the eye is all the more remarkable. We know that the original was of modest dimensions and that it has been cased and re-cased at least seven times. Yet surely the fluid line of the stupa's main curve and the perfect proportions in relation to its moulding and lotus petals reflect a single conception.

The Approach to the Shwedagon Pagoda You will not have been in Rangoon long before you catch a glimpse of the Shwedagon. Thereafter from far and near it keeps floating into one's vision, so before you actually get there you are likely to have experienced several facets of its personality. The most dramatic approach to the pagoda is via the southern tree-lined Pagoda Road. From the far end the stupa beckons, illuminated by the tropical sun. To the left one passes the memorial to U Thant, former Secretary-General of the United Nations, and a memorial to Queen Supayalat, Burma's last queen. Further on to the right is a small pagoda which marks the original southern entrance to the Shwedagon. The energetic pilgrim should alight here at the foot of the southern staircase. The majority, however, will perhaps follow the road to the right and alight from their transport half-way up.

A Visit to the Shwedagon At this stage it is possible to enter a lift which will transport you to the pagoda's terraces. (Those wishing to use a camera must pay a fee of five *kyats* at the kiosk just to the right of the lift exit.) But how much more exciting it is for the visitor to allow the pagoda to reveal its secrets at its own pace. One should enter the southern staircase here. After a moment the eyes become

Shwedagon Stupa Treasure

The gold of the Shwedagon's stupa is indeed real. From the base up to the mouldings it is gilded. About every ten years it is re-gilded using 28,000 packets of gold leaf. From the top of the mouldings to the top of the 'banana bud', the stupa is sheathed by 13,153 pure gold plates each a foot square (one can calculate their total weight at about 60 tons, with a theoretical value at today's prices of some US$750 million!). The *hti* or umbrella at the top of the stupa is an iron-tiered structure plated with 215 kilograms (470 pounds) of pure gold hung with gold and silver bells and 'diverse items of jewellery', all of which creates the gentle jingle one hears from below. The weather vane at its very top is decorated with 1,000 diamonds weighing in total 278 carats and 1,383 other precious and semi-precious stones. This splendour is in turn topped by a diamond orb, some 25 centimetres (10 inches) in diameter and studded with 4,351 diamonds weighing 1,800 carats, the summit of the orb being crowned with a single 76-carat diamond. This astonishing accumulation of treasure has been built up over the centuries, much of it predating historical records. The major gold plating was carried out from 1768 to 1774 during the reign of King Hsinbyushin. The present *hti* was given by King Mindon in 1871, although he was never permitted by the British to see the Shwedagon. The pagoda is also the recipient of frequent private donations as well as endowments to provide for its upkeep.

Other than the removal of the Dhammazedi Bell by Felipe de Brito in 1612, the attempted removal of the Singu Min Bell by the British in 1825, and later the vandalism by the British invaders during the second Anglo-Burmese War (1852), there does not seem to be any record of significant thefts from this storehouse of Buddhist merit.

accustomed to the sudden darkness, the nose to the heady scent of *thanaka*, jasmine and sandalwood, and one finds oneself in an Aladdin's cave of 'Nirvana goods' — stalls with fantastic head-dresses, Buddha images, religious stones, gold leaf, monks' paraphernalia, lacquerware, *thanaka* wood cosmetics and, near the head of the stairs, layer upon layer of fragrant flowers waiting to be bought as offerings. The stairway crosses the pagoda's former fortifications, a now dried-up moat (until 1928 a wooden draw-bridge was hoisted every night). On reaching the top, one encounters a glittering shrine hall dedicated to Konagamana, the second Buddha. Turning to the left — pilgrims must always go clockwise, keeping the pagoda to the right — the full splendour of the pagoda is revealed. First, the golden mass of the lower stupa's bell shape (Buddha's inverted begging bowl) commands attention; then the eyes are drawn towards the banana bud, past the delicate tracery of the *hti*, its myriad jewels twinkling in the sun, and bells gently stirring in the breeze.

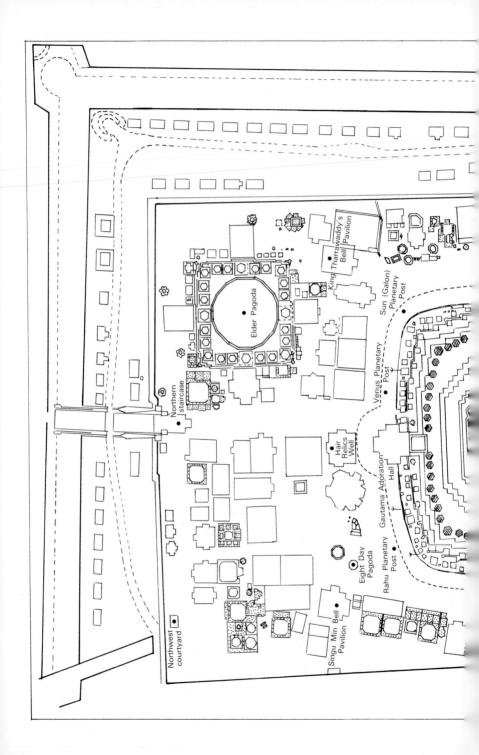

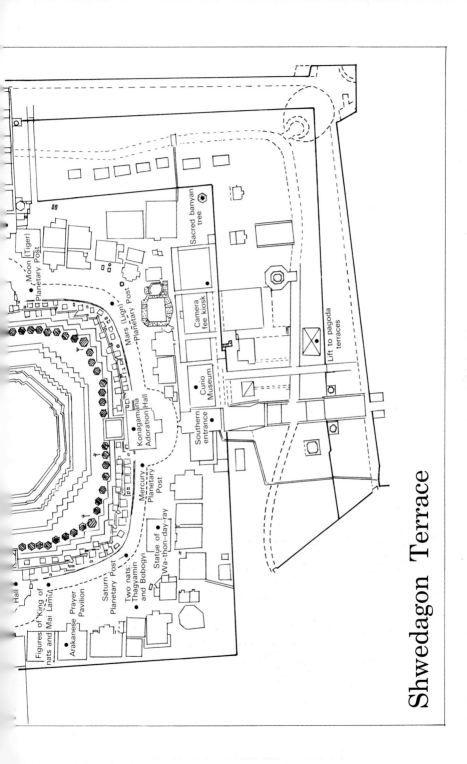

Shwedagon Terrace

Moon (Tiger)
Planetary Post

Mars (Lion)
Planetary Post

Konagamana
Adoration Hall

Mercury
Planetary
Post

Sacred banyan
tree

Camera
fee kiosk

Curio
Museum

Southern
entrance

Lift to pagoda
terraces

Figures of King of
nats and Mai Lamu

Arakanese Prayer Pavilion

Saturn
Planetary Post

Two nats:
Thagyamin
and Bobogyi

Statue of
Wa-thon-day-ray

Hall

All around the Shwedagon one finds the calm activity of a religious village, for a great pagoda is the focus of secular as well as religious life, none more than the Shwedagon. Businessmen come to worship and then settle down to negotiate a deal, students to read, families to picnic — all gaining inspiration from their surroundings.

The pagoda platform occupies an area of 5.6 hectares (14 acres), covered with buildings of all shapes and sizes. Some hug the base of the stupa, others the outer rim. Immediately on the right after the shrine hall sits the elephant of the 'Mercury Planetary Post', guardian of those born on Wednesday morning. Many visit the pagoda to pay respects to their planetary post. In Burmese astrology the week has eight days — Wednesday being split into morning and evening — with each day represented both by a planet and an animal. 'The planet of a man's birthday will be the main guardian of his fate but at each particular period of a man's life a particular planet throws upon him its painful or its beneficial influence.' *The thin-bon-gyi* (the 'Great Basket of Learning', i.e., the Burmese alphabet) is divided between the eight days of the week, and it is customary to incorporate into a person's name the letters corresponding to his birthday. At the eight cardinal points round the base of the pagoda are the planetary posts. Thus if born on a Sunday, one takes flowers, lights a candle and pours water over the image in the 'Sunday corner'.

Near the Mercury Planetary Post, looking up at the Great Stupa, is a stone statue of Wa-thon-day-ray, the guardian angel of the earth. When Mara, 'the evil one', engulfed the world in a great fire, it is said the guardian angel first soaked her long tresses of hair (which can be seen wound round her body) and then wrung them out to extinguish the blaze, thus saving the Buddha, who was meditating under the *bo* tree. On the southwest corner is the planetary post of Saturn; this is for the Saturday born and is represented by a *naga*. Continue a few steps and on the opposite side of some trees are two *nat* figures in a glass case. On the left is Thagyamin, King of the *Nats*, and on the right Bobogyi, Guardian *Nat* of the Pagoda. In front of them stand a row of gongs; when a pilgrim's prayers are said he will strike the deep-throated gong, then the ground, 'to call upon all living things in the 31 worlds to share in the merit of the good deed.'

The next pavilion — known as the Arakanese Prayer Pavilion — contains some of the finest wood carving in the pagoda. Opposite this hall under the white umbrellas of royalty stand the figures of Mai Lamu and the King of the *Nats*. Legend tells us that they were the parents of King Ukkalapa, who enshrined Buddha's hair in the pagoda.

The western staircase and Kassapa Adoration Hall were both

gutted by fire in 1931 and re-built four years later. The Two-Pice Tazaung (pavilion) which heads the staircase is so named as the merchants in Rangoon's main market each donated two *pice* (a half-penny in contemporary British money) a day for the reconstruction of the staircase and hall. The main image in the adoration hall is that of Kassapa, the Third Buddha. Just north of the adoration hall is the Jupiter Planetary Post, for the Thursday-born, whose symbol is a rat. On to the northwest corner there stands the Tuskless Elephant representing the planetary post of Rahu (the mythical planet for Wednesday afternoon). Standing alone just north of the planetary post is the small 'Eight-day Pagoda'. Around its base are eight niches, each containing a Buddha. Sitting astride each niche is the figure of the relevant animal or bird, each one representing a planet, a day of the week and a direction of the compass. The last explains the apparently haphazard sequence in which the planetary posts are arranged around the pagoda. (For example, Wednesday is followed by Saturday then Thursday). The Singu Min Bell hangs in a pavilion to the west of the Eight-day Pagoda. This splendid bell was cast between 1775 and 1779 and weighs 23 tons. In 1825 the British attempted to steal the bell; they hauled it down and onto the Rangoon River where it sank. Years later the Burmese managed to recover it with the help of bamboo rafts. From a small, charming courtyard behind the Singu Min Bell, in the northwest corner of the terrace, you get not only a wonderful view of Rangoon city, but also a superb view of the Great Stupa itself.

From here, walk along the northern wall to the northern staircase. This staircase leads to Heroes' Hill where General Aung San, the architect of Burma's independence, and other national martyrs are buried.

Turning back towards the main stupa, immediately on your left is a golden pagoda, the Elder or Naungdawgyi Pagoda. This marks the spot where the Sacred Hair Relics were first placed prior to being washed and then enshrined in the main pagoda. Continue walking towards the main stupa, and just in front of the northern adoration hall dedicated to Gautama the Fourth Buddha stands the Hair Relics Well (Sandawdwin Tazaung). This well is supposed to be fed by the Irrawaddy and so rises and falls with the tide. Tucked in on the east side of the Gautama Adoration Hall is the planetary post of Venus, for the Friday-born, and symbolized by the mole or guinea pig. In the northeast corner of the terrace is a second bell pavilion, which houses the massive Maha Titthadaganda bell, cast by King Tharrawaddy in 1841. At the base of the pagoda on the northeast side stands a galon (bird), the planetary post of the sun and therefore for the Sunday-born. The shrine hall facing the eastern stairway has been rebuilt several times and was last renovated in 1968. This hall is dedicated to

Kakusandha, the First Buddha. Beside the hall is the planetary post of the moon, for those born on Monday, with the tiger being their mascot. The last planetary post, that of Mars, stands on the southeast base of the stupa: it is represented by a lion and is for the Tuesday-born.

From the southeast planetary post, weave through the various pavilions to the southeast corner of the terrace, where there is a sacred banyan (*ficus religioso*, or *bo* tree), supposedly a descendant by a cutting from the original tree under which Gautama Buddha attained enlightenment. It is ceremoniously washed every May at the full moon. There is a fine view from this corner and on a clear day it is possible to see the Kyaik-Khauk Pagoda at Syriam. Just before arriving once more at the head of the southern stairway there is a small museum to the left of the main promenade, which contains an assortment of artefacts donated by devotees.

Dawn or dusk are the best times to visit the Shwedagon, the misty glow of the sun softening the timeless lines of the golden spire. Pilgrims, lost in prayer and acts of devotion, are engulfed in a dream-like haze. Wandering the marble terraces, warm to the feet following the day's fierce sun, and marvelling at the splendour, Ralph Fitch, a 16th-century merchant adventurer, came to a simple conclusion: 'It is the fairest place, as I suppose, that is in the world.'

The Royal Lake

An excellent place from which to view the Shwedagon is the Royal or Karaweik Lake. On the east side of the lake is the Karaweik stone boat. This is a relatively recent copy of a royal barge, and is used as a restaurant where rather good Burmese variety shows are performed every evening.

Zoological Gardens

On the southern side of the Royal Lake are the Zoological Gardens. The animals, mostly indigenous species, are well looked after. The elephants are often to be seen taking an afternoon stroll around the lake. Several years ago the Natural History Museum building, also on the lake, was converted into a hotel and the exhibits moved here to the Zoological Gardens.

Christian Cemetery

At the southwest corner of the Royal Lake is the Christian Cemetery. Like most colonial cemeteries it is a grand affair, but has fallen into disrepair. Recently, however, a committee has been formed to oversee its maintenance and return it to its former beauty.

Sule Pagoda

In the heart of Rangoon stands the Sule Pagoda: a beautiful octagonal golden stupa with a legend dating back 2,000 years. In what must be one of Burma's strangest contradictions, this statement of Buddhist calm acts as a traffic island at one of the city's few busy intersections! Two missionary monks are said to have travelled to Thaton in south-east Burma carrying a hair relic of the Buddha. The King of Thaton gave them permission to build a pagoda on the site of the present Sule Pagoda (near to the sacred Singuttara Hill) in which to enshrine the hair. The pagoda was long known as Kyaik Athok, literally 'pagoda containing hair relic' in the Mon language. The name Sule probably refers to the Sule *nat*, the guardian spirit of Singuttara Hill. It was to the Sule *nat* that the two merchant brothers, Taphussa and Bhallika, appealed to show them the sacred Singuttara Hill on their quest to found the Shwedagon Pagoda.

National Museum

From the Sule Pagoda it is a pleasant stroll to the National Museum. Walk south along Sule Pagoda Road: on the left is a small park named after Maha-Bandoola, the commander-in-chief of the Burmese army who led the raid into Assam which resulted in the first Anglo- Burmese war. He later (in 1826) defended unsuccessfully the Shwedagon Pagoda against the British force and died in the attempt — by all accounts, from both Burmese and British sources, a remarkable and brave soldier. The north and east sides of the square are dominated by fine colonial buildings, and the City Hall has a distinct Burmese flavour. Walk another block down to the Rangoon River, turn left, then left again up Pansodan (Phayre) Street, and the museum is on the right.

The ground floor exhibits are all paraphernalia from the last two kings of Burma — royal regalia, clothes, furniture, the *pièce de résistance* being the Lion Throne. When King Theebaw was exiled to Calcutta in 1886 the throne was housed in the Calcutta Museum. It was returned once more in 1948 when Burma was granted her independence from the British. On the first floor is a room of prehistoric relics and another showing pieces from Pagan. Though small, the National Museum is interesting and certainly worth a visit. In particular, some of the royal jewellery is quite beautiful. The museum is not air-conditioned so ask the custodian to turn on the fans.

The museum is open 10 am to 3 pm Sunday to Thursday; 1 pm to 3 pm Saturday; closed Friday.

Strand Hotel

A mere five minutes' walk from the museum is the Strand Hotel — a perfect spot for the tired traveller to regain lost energy over a glass of cool fresh lime and to muse on what colonial life must have been like. 'Leading Hotel in the East . . . patronized by royalty, nobility and distinguished personages' reads the advertisement in Murray's 1911 Handbook; it then goes on to list some of the hotel's distinguished guests, including HIH the Grand Duke Cyril of Russia and the Hon Mr William H Taft, President of the USA. The Strand, a handsome white stucco turn-of-the-century building, originally belonged to the Sarkie Brothers, also proprietors of Raffles ('the Savoy of the East') in Singapore.

Today the Strand's persona is that of a gentle maiden aunt in reduced circumstances. Everything is a little shabby. The reception rooms are fine lofty spaces somewhat devoid of furniture. As one sits, drink in hand, while an overhead fan gently disturbs the air, it is easy to imagine groups of elegant ladies seated in rattan chairs, the accompanying 'men in white drill or pongee silk, a great deal of laughter and pleasant conversation'. The dining room is perhaps least changed from those colonial days. The menu still boasts porridge for breakfast, excellent fish and chips for lunch, with lobster Thermidor followed by a soufflé for dinner. The bedrooms are large with comfortable beds, the furniture a little dilapidated. Although the air-conditioning sometimes works, a PhD in plumbing would be useful to cope with the bathroom eccentricities. The lifts are charming wrought-iron cages which are surprisingly efficient. Beside the reception desk is a lost-and-found cupboard containing an interesting assortment of colonial left-behinds, including a tortoiseshell pince-nez and an ivory fan.

A stay at the Strand, with its fading Somerset Maugham charm, is hard to resist for collectors of the 'period piece' (for whom its central location is an added bonus). For less committed nostalgia seekers a visit at least is highly recommended.

Botataung Pagoda

Close to the Rangoon River stands the Botataung Pagoda. The original building, which was bombed by the allies in 1943, had yet another legendary '2,000-year history'. Hairs of the Buddha are said to

have been escorted from India by 1,000 military officers ('Bota-taung'). When the pagoda was rebuilt after the war it was constructed with a hollow inside so the visitor can walk into the stupa; it is entirely lined with glass mosaics, a sort of oriental Hall of Mirrors. Many of the ancient relics have been put into glass cases — though not, of course, the sacred hair relics, which remain enshrined in the fabric of the pagoda itself.

Bogyoke Aung San Market

For market lovers this one is a pure delight. It lies just southwest of the Railway Station (itself a fine building), is crowded with stalls selling *longyis*, mother-of-pearl, lacquer, hats packaged in exquisite turquoise boxes, antique baskets, and with mobile food hawkers selling coconut with jelly. At the north end of the market is the food section, and flanking the southern end are some regular shops. At 1 and 2 Bogyoke Market is a particularly agreeable lacquerware shop. Its designs are slightly different from those elsewhere — simpler and more attuned to Western tastes — and of course proportionately more expensive. The original sign, long and Victorian, with beautiful script, now hangs inside, as signs longer than 69 centimetres (2 feet 2 inches) are liable to government tax. (Incidentally, green shop signs denote government-owned shops.)

Chauk Htat Gyi Pagoda

Just north of the Shwedagon in Shwegondaing Road is a 72-metre (230-foot) reclining Buddha. Sculpted little more than ten years ago at a cost of some 500,000 *kyats* from public donations, it provides a perfect example of how much money Burmese society continues to pour into Buddhism. This particular image holds no special charm, but is remarkable for its size.

Maha Pasana Guha

North of Rangoon University and the Inya Lake is the Maha Pasana Guha, an extraordinary artificial cave constructed in 1954 to hold the Sixth Buddhist Synod, convened by U Nu, first Prime Minister of the Union of Burma. The cave was built by volunteer labour in the space of just 14 months. It can hold up to 10,000 people. The Sixth Buddhist Synod brought the Institute for Advanced Buddhistic Studies into being with aid from the Ford Foundation. This institute is tackling the first-ever translation into English of the entire Buddhist canon. U Nu, now in his 80s, is still involved with this mammoth project.

Kaba Aye Pagoda

Kaba Aye literally means 'world peace' and this pagoda, which stands in the same compound as the 'Great Cave', was built to commemorate the Sixth Buddhist Synod.

Around Rangoon

Pegu

Pegu, once the capital of the powerful Mon Kingdom but now a charming backwater, still has many interesting things to see. Situated 80 kilometres (50 miles) northeast of Rangoon, it makes an ideal day trip or an overnight stop on the way to Kyaik-Tiyo.

The Mons (Talaings) are thought to have first settled in the Pegu area around the end of the sixth century. Pegu was then on the coast and soon developed into a prosperous port. After 1287 and the collapse of the First Burmese Empire, a Mon kingdom was again formed, this time with its capital at Martaban. But King Byinnya-U, the second Mon king, realized the strategic importance of Pegu and transferred his capital there in 1365. So began Pegu's golden era. The 'great city called Pegu' was frequented by Western travellers and merchants. In 1541 Burmese again overthrew the Mon kingdom and formed the Second Burmese Empire. This time Pegu was made the capital of the whole of Burma. The city retained this status for the next 91 years, after which Ava, on the banks of the Irrawaddy, was thought to be a more central vantage point with better communications — Pegu's harbour was silting up — and so the capital was moved north. Apart from from the years 1740 to 1757, when another Mon kingdom briefly came into existence around Pegu, the city receded into obscurity. Indeed, it had been destroyed by King Alaungpaya in 1757. In 1852 it came into the hands of the British as a result of the second Anglo-Burmese war.

The Road to Pegu

Some 40 minutes' drive from the centre of Rangoon is the **British War Cemetery** at **Htaukkyan**. A vast circular colonnade bearing the names of those whose remains were never found forms the centre of the cemetery. One of the names inscribed here is that of The Marquis of Dufferin and Ava (the great grandson of the Viceroy who annexed Burma in 1856), who ironically was killed at Ava. In all, some 27,000 Allied soldiers are buried here. The cemetery is a calm, peaceful place and is beautifully tended by the Commonwealth War Graves Commission.

Close to the cemetery is a curious shrine, a glass mosaic *naga* wrapped around a Buddha image.

Sights in Pegu

Shwemawdaw Pagoda

The fine Shwemawdaw Pagoda stands 117 metres (374 feet) — taller than the Shwedagon — overlooking the city of Pegu. Its history, the usual mixture of legend and fact, tells of two brothers who returned from India with two sacred hairs given them by Gautama Buddha, which they enshrined in a pagoda. Later this pagoda was enlarged several times: in AD 825 to a height of 24 metres (81 feet); in 1385 to 86 metres (277 feet) by King Dhammazedi (who also added a tooth of the Buddha to the relics); and in 1796 King Bodawpaya raised it slightly, to 87 metres (279 feet), and donated a new *hti*. Earthquakes have dealt savagely with the Shwemawdaw. The most devastating was in 1930, when the pagoda was flattened. It was not rebuilt until the 1950s, when it reached its present height. In design the 'Great Golden Pagoda' is not dissimilar to that of the Shwedagon. One approaches up a covered stairway and emerges onto a spacious terrace, with the stupa towering above.

Hinthagon

Just east of the Shwemawdaw Pagoda is Hinthagon Hill and Pagoda. This is supposed originally to have been an island (which later became joined to the mainland) large enough for a pair of *hinthas* (mythical birds) to perch one on top of the other, marking the place of Pegu's original settlement.

Shwethalyaung

This magnificent reclining Buddha, 56 metres (180 feet) long and 18 metres (56 feet) high, dates from AD 994. Resting on glass mosaic pillows, the face achieves serenity despite rather florid painted lines and the shed in which it lies. The Shwethalyaung Buddha was discovered abandoned in 1881 when the British were constructing the Rangoon−Pegu railway. It was restored, and then some time later the unfortunate shed was erected.

Kalyani Sima

The original Kalyani Sima was a monks' ordination hall constructed by King Dhammazedi in 1476. It was destroyed by King Alaungpaya in 1757, but was rebuilt in the 1950s.

Mahazedi Pagoda

This is another pagoda which suffered the ravages of both King
Alaungpaya and the 1930 earthquakes. King Bayinnaung built this
'Great Pagoda' in 1560 to house the Kandy Tooth (of Buddha) which
he thought he had acquired, only to discover that it was a fake. The
original was still in Ceylon. The tooth was later removed by the
victorious Burmese and temporarily installed in a pagoda in Toungoo.
It was finally enshrined along with the begging bowl in which it sits, in
the Kaunghmundaw Pagoda in Sagaing.

Kyaikpun

As you leave Pegu on the Rangoon Road there is a most extraordinary
sight — four enormous Buddhas sit back-to-back against a central
square pediment. This statue of the Four Buddhas of the present world
cycle is again part of King Dhammazedi's immense building
programme. Dhammazedi was a deeply religious man and only left the
monkhood when appointed king by Queen Shinsawbu, who donated
her weight in gold to the Shwedagon Pagoda. King Dhammazedi built
the 28-metre (90-foot) high Buddhas in 1476, but the 1930 earthquake
badly damaged the Buddha on the west side.

Kyaik-Tyo Pagoda

Kyaik-Tyo Pagoda is about 65 kilometres (40 miles) east of Pegu on
the railway line to Moulmein. It is one of Burma's most spectacular
pagodas but is a destination sometimes in and sometimes out of
bounds. Sir George Scott sets the scene well: 'The boulder stands on
the extreme verge of the bare rock and hangs over it as if a gust of
wind or a few extra pounds added would make it topple over and crash
down the dizzy height far away into the green valley below.' It is on
this huge boulder that the Kyaik-Tyo is precariously perched.
According to legend, the boulder is held safe by the strength of yet
another strand of Buddha's hair which is enshrined in the pagoda. The
legend tells that on one of Buddha's visits to earth, 'on the occasion of
teaching the law to his mother', he had given a hair to a hermit, who
had kept it in his own top-knot. When the hermit was dying, his
adopted son King Tissa (whose mother was a beautiful *naga*) came to
pay his last respects. The dying hermit's last request was that the
Buddha's hair should be enshrined in a pagoda built on a rock
resembling the shape of his head. Thagyamin, the King of the *Nats*,
then helped Tissa with his search and found the perfect place for the
pagoda.

At the foot of the mountain is the Kin-pun camp, where it is
possible to stay. The walk up the hill along a wooded path dotted with

nat and Buddha images, is an arduous one. During the dry season bamboo ladders are somehow attached to the boulder to allow devotees to lay their offerings on the rock at the foot of the shrine. The view from the pagoda at the top is superb.

Syriam

For those who find they have an extra day in Rangoon either at the beginning or at the end of their trip, a trip to Syriam and its surroundings offers a microcosm of Burmese charm — the river, a sleepy former European settlement, the countryside, golden pagodas and distant views of the Shwedagon. At the 'Syriam jetty' on Pazundaung Creek one boards a charming, shabby ferry. There are two passenger decks, the sides open to the breeze, the floors crowded with people while hawkers nimbly move about the boat, a brilliant exercise in agility. The journey takes roughly 45 minutes. On arrival at Syriam either hire a jeep or a pony trap. (If you want to visit the Ye Le Paya Pagoda at Kyauktan take a jeep as it is too far for a pony trap.)

From 1600 to 1613 Syriam was the stronghold of the Portuguese adventurer, Felipe de Brito. In 1617 The East India Company sent Messrs Forrest and Stavely to Syriam, marking the beginning of Burmese-British trade. By 1647 The East India Company had built a dock and house at Syriam. It developed into a highly successful trading post with Portuguese, Dutch, French and British bases. The Burmese bought cotton goods and in return sold *ganza* (a fabric similar to organdie), rice and large Martaban jars (used to transport fresh water and grain to sea-going ships). Syriam flourished until it was destroyed by King Alaungpaya in 1756. When the British annexed Lower Burma 96 years later it was Rangoon rather than Syriam which became the main trading post.

One or two European-style buildings are the only evidence of Syriam's days as host to European traders. Today's 20,000 inhabitants are mostly involved with the oil industry or the local brewery.

Sights of Syriam

Kyaik-Khauk and Paidahgyi Pagodas
A few miles south of the town up on a hill stands the Kyaik-Khauk Pagoda, a golden pagoda with lines reminiscent of the Shwedagon. The graves of two Burmese writers, Natshingaung and Padethayaza, are to be found just beside the pagoda. Nearby is the Paidahgyi Pagoda which contains a large Buddha. The building's glass mosaic pillars sparkle jauntily in the sunlight.

Kyauktan Pagoda (Ye Le Paya)

If one continues on this road going south, some 21 kilometres (13 miles) from Syriam one enters the village of Kyauktan. Walk through the market — a particularly attractive and thriving one — take a left turn, and there in front of you in the middle of the river, is a golden pagoda. Beside the little jetty are stalls piled high with flowers and eugenia sprigs for pilgrims to take across to the pagoda. Also on sale are strings of rice cracker balls, with which to feed the large and greedy catfish which swim around the island. A small boat will cross to Ye Le Paya (literally: 'in the middle of the water'). The picture as a whole is magnificent, the glistening gold of the stupa constrasted by the brown water and the dark green of the palm trees.

Mandalay

For the wind is in the palm trees, an' the temple-bells
they say:
Come you back to Mandalay,
Where the old Flotilla lay...

In fact Kipling never went to Mandalay (hence his reference to its non-existent palm trees) but he did capture the romance, mystery and intrigue which the name conjures up.

Although relatively youthful as Burmese cities go (built between 1857 and 1859), Mandalay is indeed worthy of its exotic reputation. The 'Gem City' was the scene both of incredible splendour and of appalling cruelty. In 1879, during the staging of a three-day *pwe* for his subjects, King Theebaw had 80 of his close relatives murdered because he thought they were conspiring to depose him, while noisy music helped deafen the sound of butchery. Enclosed in red velvet bags (red velvet to mask and absorb the blood, the sight of which would have horrified the Burmese) these royal corpses were then deposited in the Irrawaddy.

Today Mandalay has settled down and, with a population of approximately 600,000, is Burma's second largest city. It continues to be an important Buddhist centre, not only boasting possession of the much fought over Mahamuni Image (see page 31) but also the Kuthodaw Pagoda and the sacred Peshawar Relics. Mandalay is also the main market town for Upper Burma, a place for the hill tribe peoples to gather and the gateway to the mountain strongholds of the Shans and Kachins. The overland trade route to China also begins at Mandalay.

Mandalay's magic is not immediately apparent: for most of the year the town is hot and dusty, and for the rest chilly and damp. The majority of houses are wooden, with the occasional rather grand stucco mansion, a remnant of colonial days. The city has a spacious feel — each home has its earthern yard, either front or back. The Burmese are inveterate gardeners: lush bougainvillaeas tumble over fences, their startling pinks and oranges glowing against the dust brown of the houses. But only the Palace walls and a number of religious monuments survive to remind us of Mandalay's days as Burma's capital.

Unlike Rangoon, Moulmein or Taunggyi where so much evidence of colonialism lingers, Mandalay feels purely Burmese. For the traveller it is the centre of a vast amount to see: nearby are the former capitals of Ava, Amarapura and Sagaing, as well as the interesting towns of Mingun and Maymyo. In fact Mandalay and its surroundings are worthy of a week's visit in themselves. Sadly, however, it is often relegated merely to a single day's sightseeing.

History of Mandalay

In 1853 King Mindon ascended the Lion Throne of Upper Burma. (Following the first and second Anglo-Burmese wars the British controlled Lower Burma.) In his capital of Amarapura on the banks of the Irrawaddy, tales reached Mindon of the growing importance of Rangoon. To restore the diminished glory of the Kingdom of Ava, he planned a new capital. Religion was cited as the ostensible reason for the move. Buddhist legend has it that, during his life on earth, the Buddha had stood with his disciple Ananda at the top of Mandalay Hill and prophesied the building of a religious city on the plain below. So by building a new capital rich in religious monuments the devout King Mindon could at the same time commemorate the 2,400th anniversary of the Buddha's death and fulfil the prophecy, providing the British with a reminder of his power.

The chief monks and soothsayers agreed on a site to the south of Mandalay hill, not too near the river. This suited Mindon excellently for in his palace at Amarapura 'the noise of the foreign steamers disturbed the royal repose.' Plans were drawn up (the original, a beautiful scroll with the buildings painted in red and gold, can be seen in the Print Department of the India Office Library in London), and in June 1857 the move from Amarapura commenced. King Mindon took up residence in a temporary palace at the foot of Mandalay Hill.

Historians do not agree whether or not Mindon actually had a number of his subjects buried alive under the four corners of the city's foundations. (The basis of this age-old Burmese practice was that the victims' spirits would protect the city from its enemies.) If indeed he did, the antidote did not prove effective against the British, who overran Mandalay in 1886. By 1859 the 'Gem City' was fully inhabited, a royal proclamation having decreed that all citizens of Amarapura were to move with the king and his court (the Chinese merchants were the only ones to refuse). 1879 saw the death of King Mindon and the accession of his son Theebaw.

The new king — Burma's last — was a weak creature, entirely under the control of his shrewish queen Supayalat and her mother. For statesmanship or the welfare of his subjects Theebaw cared little, although he was a devout Buddhist. The royal couple lived an idle, decadent life in their gilded palace. Meanwhile, the Anglo-French conflict reached its climax with the annexation of Mandalay by the British in 1885. On 29 November the king and queen departed from their palace by ox-cart. Remaining at least true to her thick-skinned character, the remarkable Supayalat seemed as unimpressed by the ignominy of her downfall as she had been oblivious to her royal obligations during her years of power. Arriving at the Irrawaddy

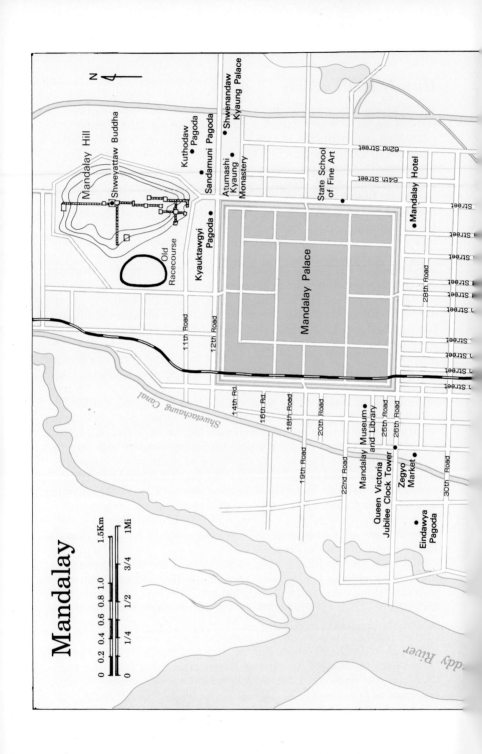

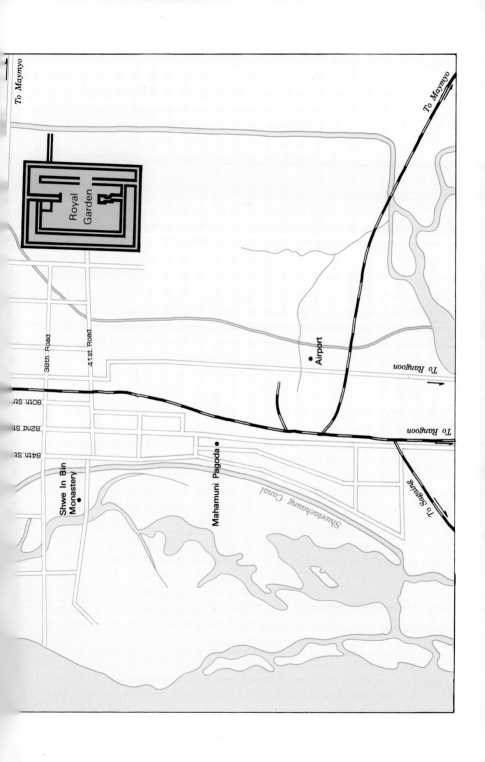

quayside on her journey into exile, she leaned out of the cart holding up her cheerot, whereupon 'there was a general rush to supply her with a box of matches. Smiling, the Queen accepted a light from a delighted Tommy.'

The City of Gems was to see many changes. The Lord of the White Elephant, deprived of his kingdom and palace, soon died. With Burma now a province of British India, the Mandalay Palace was renamed Fort Dufferin, after the then Viceroy of India who was later to become the Marquis of Dufferin and Ava. The fort was used as the administrative headquarters, while the Hall of Audience became the church, an altar being set up in front of the Lion Throne.

For the next 50 years the city prospered, river trade boomed, and when the railways were extended into Upper Burma, Mandalay served as the northern terminus. Although Mandalay enjoyed a calm unknown in the time of Theebaw, the excitement and intrigue of former days was missed by some: Sir George Scott lamented, 'There are no agreeable scallywags. There are Cooks tourists instead during the three cool months of the year.'

April 1942 brought an end to the calm with the arrival of the invading Japanese army. For three years they used Mandalay as their northern headquarters, and Allied planes repeatedly bombed the city. As the majority of the buildings were wooden, the resulting fires were horrendous. In March 1945, Gurkha and British troops stormed the city and, after fierce fighting, took the Japanese strongholds of Fort Dufferin and Mandalay Hill. During their occupation the Japanese had built an intricate web of concrete lined tunnels in the pagoda-covered hill. Unfortunately, the palace did not survive the Allied attack. 'The palace had been burnt down,' Field Marshall Slim recalled, 'Whether fired by our shelling and bombing, although we had tried to avoid it, or by the Japanese to destroy the stores they had in it, I do not know.'

Since then Mandalay has not managed to escape further fires, which break out in different parts of the city with distressing frequency, the worst of which occurred in the spring of 1985.

Sights in Mandalay

Mandalay Palace

The Hall of Audience with its seven tiered golden spire stood at the 'Centre of the Universe', as the palace was called, surrounded by the other throne halls: the Duck Throne, where foreigners were received; the Elephant and Deer Thrones, employed for purposes relating to the Lord White Elephant; and the Lily Throne, where the Chief Queen received guests on feast days. In all there were 133 apartments (King Mindon had 53 recognized wives and many concubines) within the massive pink crenellated walls. The palaces were built of teak, lacquered, gilded and, in some instances, such as the Glass Palace, entirely covered with mosaics of coloured glass. To a Westerner, there was however an eyesore — the corrugated iron roofs 'the invention of which must rank among the major crimes of the Western world'. But to Mindon they were both practical and almost the ideal colour (traditionally a king was supposed to live beneath silver roofs), and they were reminiscent of the Great Khan's fabled palaces of shining roofs. The lotus covered moat was spanned by white bridges leading to the 12 gates. There were three gates on each of the three-kilometre (two-mile) sides of the square. Guarding every gate-top was a delicate wooden spire (*pyathat*). The main entrance was the eastern gate which was reserved exclusively for the use of the king. Foreigners and condemned men were relegated to the inauspicious western gate. Two little tricks were employed to remind foreigners of court protocol. First, the lintel on the western gate was so low that the visitor had to bend to enter. Second, nails were placed in the floor of the Duck Throne Room, their points surreptitiously poking up through the polished teak boards. It being *de rigueur* to remove footwear in the palace, this forced wary barefooted foreigners to remain bent in supplication.

To visit the 2,000 acres of the palace grounds today a guide is required as units of the Burmese Army are stationed within its walls. There is a scale model of the palace as it was but little remains today of the actual buildings. Some foundations, King Theebaw's palace (without its roof), the original plinth of the Lion Throne (the throne itself is now in the Rangoon Museum), and a reconstructed version of the Glass Palace are all that remain of the last and possibly most splendid manifestation of the Burmese monarchy. Wandering among the ruins and scrub jungle, visitors should equip themselves with a keen sense of imagination to visualize the exotic elegance, the other-wordly calm, the tragi-comic pride and intrigue of the court of King Mindon.

Shwenandaw Kyaung

The only palace building to survive World War II intact is the Shwenandaw Kyaung. King Theebaw thought it was inauspicious (his father King Mindon had died in the building) and, on his accession in 1879, had it moved to its present location east of the palace not far from the foot of Mandalay Hill. This beautiful building is surrounded by a teak platform supported on wooden pillars topped with marble lotus flowers. The outer walls are finely carved, some panels decorated with mythical animals, others dancing figures, the rest a lace-like trellis carving of vines and flowers. The weather, which has given the teak a soft greyish-brown patina, has dealt savagely with the reliefs, many of which are crumbling and pitted. Inside the building are two massive halls. The main hall contains a copy of the Lion Throne, a Buddha image commissioned by Theebaw with the features of his father, and a gold couch that Theebaw is said to have used during meditative visits here. This room retains echoes of its courtly past. Each massive pillar is a single trunk of teak still showing remnants of vermilion, lacquer, gold and filigree decorations. Around the ceiling base are fine carvings of *nats* worshipping the Buddha; the ceiling itself is painted with golden sparrows. This ornamentation is lit rather charmingly by a single neon strip complete with dangling cobwebs.

Atumashi Kyaung

The Atumashi Kyaung (Incomparable Monastery) stands beside the Shwenandaw Kyaung and is today a shell of stairs and foundations. Completed in 1878, it was the last great religious edifice constructed by King Mindon. It housed four valuable sets of the Tripitaka and a nine-metre (30-foot) high standing Buddha with a huge diamond set into the forehead. On the evening of 29 November 1885, the night following King Theebaw's surrender to General Prendergast, Mandalay was over-run by dacoits and the diamond was stolen — some say by British soldiers. It has never been recovered. In 1890 the monastery was destroyed by fire, but what remains of the stucco carving is quite fine.

Kuthodaw Pagoda (Maha Lawkamazin)

In 1857 King Mindon built the Kuthodaw Pagoda, a copy of the Shwezigon Pagoda in Pagan, which itself had been commenced in the reign of King Anawrahta. At the entrance to the pagoda visitors are gently reminded of Burmese custom: 'Prohibited Footwearing Cycling Umbrella Holding'. A long, cool corridor leads to the pagoda itself which stands in a beautiful setting surrounded by little white stupas and huge, spreading 'star flower' trees. As so often in Burma, the simple beauty of the stupa is marred by *ad hoc* wiring which supplies unattractive neon light (as opposed to the charming variety in the Shwenandaw) on the *hti* (umbrella) — a nightmare for keen photographers. Also typically Burmese is the mixture of religious and

secular life within the pagoda. By the entrance there are early 20th-century clockwork sideshows: climb some wooden steps, place a coin in the open mouth of a cat, and around come models of Burma's hill tribes! Kuthodaw is often named 'the biggest book in the world', for surrounding it are 729 marble slabs inscribed with the Tripitaka texts (the index is to be found beside the sideshows). In 1871 King Mindon had convened a meeting of 2,400 monks from all over Burma to discuss the Buddhist texts. After several months of deliberation a new 'authorized' version was agreed on. The texts were then carved onto the marble slabs (apparently with some mistakes). Mindon felt this would safeguard the scriptures which were otherwise highly vulnerable (as indeed proved the case of the Incomparable Monastery) for they were traditionally recorded on palm leaves.

Sandamuni Pagoda

Sandamuni is another pagoda surrounded by inscribed marble slabs, in this case housed in mini-stupas, whereas those of the Kuthodaw are in square houses with a twirl of 'icing sugar' plaster on top. These slabs record commentaries on the Tripitaka. It was to a temporary palace on this site that King Mindon moved in June 1857 from Amarapura to oversee the building of his new Golden City. The site also bears sad associations. It was here that Mindon's half brother and confidante, Crown Prince Kanaung, is buried. In gratitude for the Prince's help in overthrowing his predecessor, King Pagan Min, Mindon had made Kanaung crown prince. On 8 June 1866 two of Mindon's sons, aggrieved at being excluded from the succession, had planned to assassinate both their father and uncle. They consulted the *ponnas* (Brahmin soothsayers) who suggested as auspicious a day on which the *ponnas* knew King Mindon was to visit his temporary palace, leaving Prince Kanaung in charge. The rebel princes stormed the palace, killed Prince Kanaung, and then set off for the temporary palace intending to kill Mindon. He, however, managed to escape and return safely to the Golden City. Luckily the princes had left only a solitary guard to watch for the king, and Mindon's loyal slaves made quick work of him. This tragedy is probably the reason King Mindon failed to appoint another successor, thus making it possible for the scheming Central Queen, mother of Supayalat, to persuade the King on his deathbed to acclaim his weakling son Theebaw as successor.

Kyauktawgyi Pagoda

Att the foot of Mandalay Hill stands the Kyauktawgyi Pagoda. The covered corridor leads through a garden where images of Buddha's 80 disciples (20 on each side) stand guard, each in a little house. A painted fresco around the end of the corridor illustrates 16 dreams of King Kawsala (an Indian king and contemporary of Gautama Buddha) — premonitions which were predicted to come true on the 2,500th anniversary of the Buddha's death, which by Burmese reckoning fell in 1952. (There is much variation in the records as to when and for how long Gautama Buddha lived, though common belief is that he was born in India in 566 BC and lived 80 years.) One of the fresco panels tells of the world's women fighting for liberation. Originally King Mindon planned for this pagoda to be styled after the Ananda Pagoda in Pagan, but the finished article bears no resemblance to it. Instead of four colossal Buddha images, it houses only one. This is crafted from a single piece of the palest green marble quarried at Sagyin, some 18 kilometres (12 miles) up the Irrawaddy. It was rafted downriver to Mandalay, but there was no way to transport it over the last leg, across dry land. A canal was dug but, the story goes, there was not sufficient water to sustain the giant raft. So 10,000 conscripted labourers were ordered into the canal, thus raising the water level sufficiently to allow the great marble slab to be floated to its destination, where it was then carved into its present form. It is a beautiful image, and — for one so large — conveys profound serenity. The head is decorated with delicate gold filigree. The dress and shawl are inlaid with jewels all of which, save for the central diamond, are said to be synthetic. To remind one of the 20th century a green telephone in a padlocked box stands close by.

Mandalay Hill

Two enormous lions guard the foot of the southern staircase leading up the sacred Mandalay Hill. The best time to visit Mandalay Hill is early morning, before breakfast, avoiding the heat of the day. The view from the top is spectacular. To the south and east lies the city of Mandalay, Mindon's 'Cluster of Gems', and beyond it early morning mists roll off the huge Irrawaddy. (Sir George Scott knew this view well and noted how 'The river glitters like diamonds in the patches that catch the early sun.') If it is not too misty the Ava Bridge and the barren pagoda-crowned hills of Sagaing will be visible. To the north and west, the broad rice-growing plains meld into the Shan Hills. Of the religious monuments themselves, the first pagoda on ascending the hill contains the Peshawar Relics (now exhibited at the U Khanti Museum on the west side of Mandalay Hill). These relics are said to be three bones of the Buddha originally given to the king of Peshawar (now in Pakistan) by the great King Ashoka in around AD 235 and

passed on in turn to the Burmese Buddhist Society by the British in 1908. By then Peshawar, once a Buddhist centre, had long since become predominantly Islamic.

Further up — there are plenty of places for the weary to rest — the huge golden Shweyattaw Buddha stands guard over the city. It is here that the Buddha, accompanied by his disciple Ananda, is thought to have stood and prophesied the building of a great religious city. Before commencing his 'City of Gems' King Mindon erected this statue in memory of the Buddha's prophesy. This figure is unusual in that, unlike most Buddha images, his hands are not in the *mudra* position; rather, his right hand points to the city below.

Silk Weaving

A pleasant interlude to a pagoda-packed day is to visit the silk weavers in the street opposite the eastern entrance to Mandalay Palace. You know you are approaching the correct location when you hear the clack-clack of the looms, on which the traditional wedding *longyis* for both men and women are woven. Two girls work at each wooden loom passing the one to two hundred different bobbins to and fro as they thread them through the silk, a mirror near at hand to check the pattern. Today the silk yarn is imported from Japan, and the dye mainly from Britain; formerly vegetable dyes would have been used. One of these beautiful *longyis*, 1.1 metres (44 inches) wide and 1.8 metres (two yards) long, should cost about 1,400 to 2,200 *kyats*.

State School of Fine Art

Just south from the silk weavers' street is the State School of Fine Art. Here you can watch young hopefuls being coached in the Burmese performing arts — dance, music, puppetry and acting. The discordant crashes and wails of the music can be trying to the untrained ear, but the fluid, elegant movements of the dancers are a pleasure to behold. The Burmese are also skilled puppeteers. As in their live theatre, the acts are often based on stories from the life of Buddha and from the Ramayana (the Hindu epics).

Zegyo Market

At the centre of the town (within walking distance from the Mandalay Hotel) stands the Queen Victoria Jubilee Clock Tower, next to which is the Zegyo Market. Mandalay is the main market for the surrounding region and Zegyo is a large, bustling affair. At dawn farmers, towels wrapped around their heads to ward off the early morning chill, start arriving, carrying enormous baskets brimming with fresh produce. Considerable time and effort is spent in laying this out with each variety of merchandise in its allotted section. The resulting display provides an everyday demonstration of the Burmese sense of style and design: a pyramid of glossy tomatoes on a flat basket, a round of green chillies with young eggplants as the centrepiece and, interspersed among these brilliant colours, mounds of tea, bundles of cheroots and neat stacks of the cosmetic *thanaka* wood. *Thanaka* powder is popular as a cosmetic with women all over Burma for its astringent and cooling as well as its aesthetic qualities. As well as the fresh produce sections, manufactured consumer items, both legitimate and smuggled, are available. There is also a night market on 79th Street, on the west side of the railway yard. For the visitor who would like a memento of Burmese music this is the place to buy a tape.

Mandalay Museum and Library

To the northeast of the market, on 80th Street between 24th and 25th Streets, is the Mandalay Museum and Library. It has an interesting collection of royal garments, probably those left behind by King Theebaw and Queen Supayalat. It has a variety of ethnological exhibits, but on the whole it is not as interesting as the museum in Taunggyi.

Eindawya Pagoda

Due west of Zegyo Market is Eindawya Pagoda. It was built by King Theebaw in memory of his uncle, the former King Pagan Min, who was deposed but spared following the palace revolution of 1853. He lived out his life in a monastery on this site, eventually dying of smallpox. This golden pagoda of lovely proportions (sadly the base has recently been covered in mosaic) was built also in memory of Theebaw's only son, who died in infancy.

Logging

Well worth a visit (and not usually included on the standard itinerary) is the log-hauling operation on the banks of the Irrawaddy just north of the Mingun ferry pier. Pairs of water buffalo, yoked together, drag the vast teak logs out of the water onto the mudbank. The authoritative voice of their handler issues resounding commands as, with greater agility than their bumbling appearance might suggest, they manage to load the mud-dripping tree trunks onto aged lorries — kept functioning by methods most mechanics would not believe — for transport to the Mandalay sawmills.

Mahamuni Pagoda

Mandalay's most fabled pagoda is the Mahamuni (or Arakan) Pagoda. It was originally built in 1784 by King Bodawpaya to house the Mahamuni Image, but was destroyed by fire in 1884 and immediately rebuilt. The 3.8-metre (12.6-foot) high seated image of the Buddha has a legendary origin and a complex history (see page 31). Three times the Burmese tried to steal it from the Arakanese, but only in 1784 were they finally successful. According to an inscription in the pagoda, King Bodawpaya coaxed this Buddha image to Mandalay by the 'charm of piety'. The history books, however, tell of a bloody battle. They do not divulge how this massive sculpture was transported over the steep, pathless mountain sides. Some, to this day, ascribe the feat to supernatural powers. One hundred and twenty families accompanied the image on its long journey to Mandalay and remained to tend it. Even today the image's face is washed and teeth cleaned at 4.30 each morning — for the early riser a fascinating ritual to watch. The shape of the body is greatly distorted as each day the faithful paste on more and more little squares of gold leaf. Sometimes it is necessary to apply a thin layer of lacquer to the body to enable the gold leaf to stick, and this is done as part of the early morning ablutions. Women believers are not allowed into the inner sanctum and have to pass their gold leaf to a man dressed in white in charge of the Buddha's welfare. Another man is employed solely to collect the fallen gold leaf — reputedly as much as 2.7 kilograms (6 pounds) a year!

In a separate building to the north of the main pagoda are six bronze Khmer statues. These are all that remain of 30 bronzes also plundered from the Arakan by King Bodawpaya. One hundred and twenty years earlier the Arakanese King Razagyi had removed these very same statues from the Burmese kingdom of Pegu. The Burmese had taken them from the Siamese capital of Ayutthia, and the Siamese had in turn looted them from their original home in Angkor Wat in Cambodia in 1431. King Theebaw had the other 24 bronzes melted and cast into cannon for his fight against the British. The bronze statues are very worn, no doubt from their many arduous journeys but also from incessant handling. If one is ill, it is believed that touching the appropriate part of one of the statues will cure the corresponding organ of one's own body. A small museum is also situated in the courtyard, housing a strange mixture of royal regalia, wax models of

King Mindon, Queen Supayalat and King Theebaw, as well as a beautiful crystal bed brought from France by King Mindon at the cost of 18,000 silver coins.

Perhaps the most fascinating part of the Mahamuni Pagoda is the long, shop-filled colonnade which leads to the famed Buddha image. It was along this colonnade that sumptuous daily offerings from the royal palace used to pass. Today it hums with trade; shopkeepers ('heavenly merchants') sell every variety of 'Nirvana goods' — lacquerware, Buddha images of all shapes and sizes and the seven items of a monk's paraphernalia (three pieces of robe, one belt, one water strainer, one razor, one begging bowl, one needle and thread). Much of what one can buy here is made in the workshops on the south side of the colonnade. This is an excellent place for the keen shopper: several stores have good embroidery, both old and new. The new pieces tend to be the most expensive, so remember to bargain. This is also the best place for waxed umbrellas of all sizes. Some of the really large ones are extremely colourful.

The Artisan Guilds

Not far from the Mahamuni Pagoda, also in the south of the city, are the Artisan Guilds. In 1857 when Mandalay was being built, King Mindon set up these guilds and today they form the backbone of Burma's craft industry. On one side of the street are the alabaster and marble carvers, and the forecourt and workshops are strewn with Buddha images of different shapes, sizes and stages of completion. Opposite are the shops of the wood carvers, where one can find charming small Buddhas carved from sweet-smelling sandalwood. Several workshops specialize in 'instant antiques' — bronzes cast using the lost wax method. In the forecourt of the establishment craftsmen model while in the rear yard heaps of dry cow-dung smoulder. From these workshops emerge exquisite little bronze Buddhas, to which an instant chemical 'age patina' is then added. The finished product may well find its way onto the Thai antique market: buyer beware. Perhaps the guild's most idiosyncratic work of all is the production of gold leaf. Gold nuggets from the mines of north Burma are first flattened to paper thinness and then placed between layers of bamboo paper wrapped in deer skin (which does not stretch). In a small hut forbidden to women stand two men, each wielding a long-handled sledge-hammer. For ten minutes at a time these muscular characters pulverize the small leather packets, rendering their contents so thin and delicate that 28 grams (one ounce) of gold covers an area of about 10 square metres (12 square yards). The gold leaf will later be sold to devotees to paste onto Buddha images.

Shwe In Bin

Monasteries abound in and around Mandalay so visit only the best.
One such is the Shwe In Bin, in Pe Boke Ian Street, south of 35th
Street. This beautiful teak building (constructed some 80 years ago by
a rich Chinese jade merchant, though many of the carved panels date
from an earlier period), raised on cream stucco foundations, stands in
its own compound shaded by mature trees. Its mud floor, baked to a
soft brown, is constantly swept by the young monks. The interior is
characteristically multicultural: beautiful carved doors in the Burmese
style, Victorian crystal paraffin lamps, as well as an interesting series of
paintings depicting General Prendergast and Colonel Sladen
negotiating with court ministers prior to King Theebaw's exile.

Mandalay's Surroundings

Amarapura

Some 11 kilometres (seven miles) south of Mandalay is the town of Amarapura, the 'City of Immortals'. In its heyday a city of some 200,000 inhabitants, it now has a population of a mere 10,000. The leisurely clack-clack from the looms of the cotton and silk weavers has replaced the noisy bustle of this former capital. The town stands on slightly elevated ground which in the flood season forms a long peninsula.

History of Amarapura In 1782 King Bodawpaya, fifth son of the great Alaungpaya, ascended the Lion Throne at Ava. His passage to the throne had been sufficiently blood-stained for his *ponnas* to advise a move of capital. This was not such a radical suggestion as it would have been in the Western world. Although Burmese cities and palaces were ornate and grand, the majority of the buildings were constructed of wood and relatively easy to dismantle, move to a new site and re-assemble. So in 1783, the court was moved a short distance north to Amarapura. During its brief tenure as capital (1783−1823 and 1841−57) Amarapura hosted two British embassies, that of Captain Symes in 1795 and of Sir Henry Yule in 1855, each of which was excellently documented. Yule travelled with a cartographer, a painter and, for the first time ever for a foreign mission, an official photographer (the unforgettably named and highly competent Linneus Tripe), so we have a clear view of contemporary life in the 'City of Immortals'. The city, true to Burmese tradition, was laid out four-square, bounded by a defensive wall some four metres (12−13 feet) high with a battlemented parapet. Pagodas on the four corners still stand and are visible from U Bein Bridge.

Sights in Amarapura

Palace Ruins and Treasury

All that remains of the palace is the yellow stuccoed treasury building and the record office, which was built by King Tharrawaddi (1837−46). Formerly it had been 'crowned with the gilt pavilion which serves as a Belvedere where the king occasionally amuses himself at eventide with his spyglass.' Nearby stand the old watchtower and the tombs of King Bodawpaya and his grandson, King Bagyidaw.

Pahtodawgyi Pagoda
This white pagoda was built by King Bagyidaw in 1820. Around the pagoda's base are tablets which illustrate the Buddha's previous lives. One of the finest views of this pagoda is from the U Bein Bridge across the Taung Thaman Lake.

U Bein Bridge
At the southern end of the town, in a grove of majestic trees, forgotten pagodas crumble. Two large monasteries remain, as does the massive Taungmingyi Buddha Image erected around 1846 by Pagan Min (King Mindon's deposed brother). This image was originally exposed to the elements, but in 1949 it was roofed in. In 1847 King Pagan Min allocated funds for the building of a bridge across Taung Thaman Lake. The mayor, one U Bein, obviously had an eye for a quick penny: he appears to have pocketed the money and re-used timbers from the abandoned Ava Palace. The king saw through the ruse, however, and the mayor was charged with fraud. The bridge passes over fertile ricefields during the winter months — the lakebed stays dry long enough for two harvests. Then, in the rainy season, from the Pahtodawgyi Pagoda in the north to the Ava stream south of Amarapura, the land floods to form the Taung Thaman Lake, and the farmers become fishermen.

Kyauktawgyi Pagoda
At the far end of the U Bein Bridge, in a grove of trees, stands the Kyauktawgyi Pagoda. This is a much smaller copy of the Ananda Temple in Pagan and was built in 1847 by King Pagan Min. Instead of the Ananda's four standing Buddhas, however, it has a single seated image, and is also noted for its 19th-century murals. The amble across the bridge to the pagoda is itself worthwhile, especially during the dry season. There are plenty of places to linger and enjoy the ravishing view, to watch a farmer balance on the cross-bar of his wooden harrow, softly whispering words of encouragement to his oxen as they labour up and down the field.

Nagayon Pagoda
On the outskirts of Amarapura is a pagoda built in the shape of a *naga* (a mythical serpent) — hence its name. The body of the *naga* is wound around the back of a vaulted building, its head erect like that of a hooded cobra.

Ava

South of Amarapura is Ava, once a mighty capital and now just a sleepy village whose inhabitants specialize in making lacquerware begging bowls for monks. In 1855 Sir Henry Yule found the remains of Ava much as they are today: 'The ramparts still stand though in decay, the greater part of the interior area is a mere mass of tangled gardens and jungle.' The journey to Ava is a pleasure in itself. Just before reaching the Ava Bridge, which crosses the Irrawaddy, one leaves the main road and lurches along a dirt track, until the Myitnge River. Here one boards a flat-bottomed ferry, most probably sharing it with an ox-cart or two, bicyclists, chickens, in fact a veritable mini-Noah's Ark. (During the wet season one boards the ferry on the Irrawaddy near the Ava Bridge.) On the far side of the river one continues by pony trap, the only four-wheeled vehicle in Ava being a very elderly fire engine.

History of Ava Ava is first noted in the records in 1364, as a Shan capital. It served as capital of Upper Burma until 1634 when, during the Second Burmese Empire, it became capital of the whole of Burma. Apart from the brief move to Amarapura, Ava remained the capital until a strong earthquake in 1838 persuaded King Tharrawaddi Min and his *ponnas* the site was inauspicious and it was abandoned for good. However, right up until 1886, when the Burmese royal family went into exile to Ratanagiri, near Bombay, the 'Kingdom of Ava' continued to be the formal name of the Burmese state.

Sights in Ava

Nanmyint Watchtower
King Bagyidaw's watchtower still stands, 'as the earthquake left it, greatly out of the perpendicular and with the massive verandah and pillars round its base staggering hither and thither.'

Maha Aungmye Bonzan
This monastery is unusual in that it is totally constructed of brick and stucco and thus survived the passage of time better than most of its contemporaries. It was built in 1818 by King Bagyidaw's chief queen for the abbot, Nyaungyan Sayadaw, who was also reputed to be her lover. It is a large, pale yellow building, decorated with fine bas-reliefs of mythical animals, gargoyles and beautiful arches.

Judson Memorial
Nearby and east of Maha Aungmye Bonzan is a memorial to the

Christian missionary Dr Adoniram Judson. It was on this site that he and other Christian prisoners were held captive during the last six months of the first Anglo-Burmese war in 1826. His wife, Anne Judson, camped in 'a little filthy room half full of grain' and cared for the prisoners.

Bagaya Kyaung

Bagaya Kyaung, perhaps the most beautiful of the monasteries in the area, famous for its 267 teak pillars, is set in the middle of Le Daw Gyee, the great royal ricefields. One walks along a narrow path across the paddy to this exquisite little wooden monastery. The carving on the doors and walls is well preserved. The main hall stands on a platform apart from the monk's quarters and the other buildings. It is constructed so that there is a space between the walls and roof, which keeps the hall light and cool throughout.

Lacquerware Factory

Ava features a lacquerware factory, where the handsome black monks' begging bowls are made. In common with all Burmese crafts the ancient methods prevail — it is said that 'the supreme test of excellence for a begging bowl of lacquer is when the sides will bend in till they touch without cracking,' the construction being of woven horsehair rather than cheaper bamboo wickerwork.

Ava Bridge

Hard as it is to believe, the Ava Bridge is, at the time writing, the only bridge to span the Irrawaddy throughout its entire length. The iron rail and road bridge was built by the British in the 1930s. In 1942 part of the bridge was blown up by the British as they retreated from the advancing Japanese. It was not repaired until 1954.

Sagaing

In the 1930s the writer, Maurice Collis, stood on the eastern bank of the Irrawaddy and gazed across at Sagaing prior to taking up his post as its Deputy Commissioner. 'Behind the town with its mat and wooden houses was a cluster of yellow hills,' he wrote, 'on top of each a golden pagoda with monasteries in profusion. There bathed in sunshine, secret and still, was Buddhist Burma.' Today there are said to be no fewer than 554 monasteries, home for roughly 5,000 monks and nuns.

History of Sagaing Sagaing served as the earliest recorded but the shortest lived capital in Upper Burma. From 1315 to 1364 the Shans

made it their capital. Some 400 years later, King Alaungpaya, the final victor over the Mons and founder of the third and last Burmese Empire, moved his capital here from his native Shwebo before eventually settling in Ava. Sagaing also figured briefly in the dynastic history of another great Asian nation: the last emperor of China's Ming Dynasty is said to have lived there for a short period after fleeing the Manchu conquest of his homeland.

Holy Fish

'The fish are incarnated with a holy spirit. They swim right up the river bank, out of the water, while worshippers press gold leaf on their heads and fill their mouths with rice. Then they swim away.'

The holy fish story is one of Burma's innumerable tales of the *nats'* latest, mischievous ploys with human fate. The fish even cropped up in an early explorer's eyewitness account.

. Hunting holy fish on seven-day visas was no easy task. Sifting the rumours for facts was tougher; *everyone* in Burma, it seemed, had heard of them. *No one* had actually seen them. Only when I found myself knee-deep in the swirling, muddy water of a small river in the central Burmese plains, holding out a large compressed rice ball, and shouting politely to the spirits of the fish to rise, was my scepticism overtaken by anxious excitement. And the sight was awesome. From a huge, seemingly lifeless expanse of brown, a huge head responded obediently, pushing gaping jaws out at the knees of a small girl. Then there were a dozen of them, and village children stuffed the protruding heads with riceballs.

Village elders called all children back from the water's edge. There was much swirling amongst fish. They popped heads up to eye their benefactors, and splashed fins and tails. Suddenly there was a great surge through the water, heading for the bank. A flabby, man-sized beast clumsily thrashed its passage through the shallows and torpedoed itself up the mud flat — right out of the water.

Villagers crowded around. For several minutes the fish lay there, moving only its jaws to accommodate the balls of rice being stuffed inside. Someone pressed goldleaf to its head, though clearly it would not hold long. Another man was pouring water to stop the fish from drying. Then, as the 'holy fish' sensed need to return to its own world with its bulging mouthful, it turned, gave a few mighty mud-slinging tail thrusts, and propelled itself away.

'Should anyone dare eat a holy fish,' I was told by the villagers, 'They will certainly die or fall gravely ill. It has happened before. Everyone in this area can identify this kind of fish, and they always free them.'

—John Everingham

Sights in Sagaing

Khemathaka Convent and Lwanzedi

In his marvellous 1855 work, *Mission to Ava*, Sir Henry Yule warns, 'Readers of this narrative are probably tired of pagodas before now — but in Burma people do get very tired of pagodas.' In Sagaing take heed of this warning and enjoy the spectacular view in addition to visiting monasteries and pagodas. In the centre of Sagaing's village street is a friendly teashop; the mildly adventurous might try the sugarcane juice. (The cane is crushed by a Heath-Robinson contraption with a large iron wheel.) The teashop also provides a fine observation point from which to watch monastic life go about its unhurried business: nuns dressed in their pale pink habits with (rather fashionable-looking) long narrow sleeves, folded bleached saffron cloths shielding their shaven heads from the sun. Nuns in Burma, unlike monks, do not beg for their food, nor is it required of the Burmese female population to spend a certain length of time in a convent. Many do, however, and it is quite common to see little girls of four or five dressed in nuns' habits, often in the same establishment as an aunt or elder sister.

Once refreshed, turn left at the T-junction at the end of the village and then left again up a flight of stairs which leads to Khemathaka Convent. Continue your climb through the convent, a collection of fine teak buildings, until you come to the main stairway and turn right up the hill. Some way up on the left will be the Lwanzedi Pagoda (if lost any passer-by can show you the way). This pagoda, though in itself of no particular artistic merit, provides a superb vantage point from which to revel in the pure beauty of the surrounding countryside. Pagodas of all shapes and sizes dot the landscape. Scattered among them are fine European-style stucco buildings. Through the middle of this picture glides the Irrawaddy, beyond it the spires of Mandalay Hill gleam, and on the horizon way to the northeast the huge dark Shan Hills rise up. The picture is 'striking and beautiful in the extreme'.

Soon U Ponya Shin Pagoda

The Soon U Ponya Shin Pagoda also enjoys a splendidly elevated position, the difference being that there is a road up to it, so for those less inclined to exertion this is the place to enjoy the panorama. It stands slightly apart, however, and you will miss the pleasure of the village scene.

Kaung Hmudaw Pagoda
Ten kilometres (six miles) west from the Ava Bridge is the Kaung
Hmudaw Pagoda. Its shape is unusual for a Burmese pagoda in that it
is an enormous dome, about 275 metres (900 feet) in circumference
and 45 metres (150 feet) high, topped by a small *hti*. It was built in
1636 by King Thalon to celebrate the founding of Ava as the
kingdom's capital. Local folklore suggests that the shape represents a
certain queen's perfect breast. The pagoda is also a copy of the
Mahaceti Pagoda in Sri Lanka and is alleged to contain a tooth of the
Buddha brought from Kandy. The base of the pagoda has small *nat*-
filled niches, as well as some 800 pillars each one-and-a-half metres
(five feet) high with a niche for an oil lamp. At the November full
moon the annual Kaung Hmundaw Pagoda festival is held. As always
at festival time a market springs up around the pagoda; this one is
renowned for pottery.

Ywahtaung Village
On the return journey from the Kaung Hmudaw Pagoda to the Ava
Bridge one passes through Ywahtaung village, the home of the
silversmiths' guild. These silversmiths produce extremely fine work,
using the ornate patterns of traditional designs. The silver betel boxes,
and bowls in the shape of monks' begging bowls, which are to be found
in most Burmese homes, are likely to have come from Ywahtaung.

Monywa

The old town of Monywa lies 122 kilometres (76 miles) west of
Sagaing. Monywa earned a footnote in Burmese history as an indirect
consequence of the attempted assassination of King Mindon in 1866.
The quick-witted slave who foiled the attempt was rewarded by
Mindon, first with the appointment as his slipper bearer, and later as
governor of Monywa. One of Burma's more famous pagodas,
Thanboddhay, is here. Monywa is a centre for traditional embroidery
as well as modern work with sequins. The nearby village of Kyauk-ha
is famous for lacquer. Tourist Burma has recently opened a new hotel
here.

Mingun

History of Mingun A boat ride up the Irrawaddy to Mingun, 'King
Bodawpaya's folly', provides a delightful half-day trip from Mandalay.
Having enlarged his kingdom to include the Arakan, carried away

their prized Mahamuni Image and founded a new capital at Amarapura, King Bodawpaya set about constructing a mammoth pagoda on the western banks of the Irrawaddy. He began to build in 1790. First he built a temporary palace on Nandaw Kyun in the middle of the river opposite the site. (It was on this same island that Captain Symes was virtually imprisoned for 40 days during his second mission to Ava in 1802.) But in 1797 the king abandoned the project. There are different theories as to why: one goes that soothsayers had warned him that if the building were finished his life would end; another suggests that he went through a period of religious disbelief; a third posits perhaps the most realistic reason, that the project was immensely costly — Bodawpaya is said to have spent over 10,000 *viss* (about 17.5 tons) of silver on it. And, of course, it was hardly prudent of the monarch to be living on a small island away from his capital.

Sights in Mingun

Settawya Pagoda
From the landing stage turn left (downstream) and follow the path across a field. On the right sit the remains of the huge pagoda guardian lions. The grey stone haunches of these majestic statues are clearly definable whereas the rest is entwined with vegetation. Walk on and the Settawya Pagoda comes into view. This attractive white pagoda surrounded by huge terraces is said to be the first pagoda built by King Bodawpaya in Mingun, presumably for use whilst he was building his folly. A central staircase leads down into a vault which houses a footprint of the Buddha.

Pondawpaya Pagoda
Nearby, at the water's edge, is a scale-model of what the Mingun Pagoda would have been had it been completed. Seeing this helps one to understand the true enormity of Bodawpaya's folly.

Mingun Pagoda
An enormous pile of bricks is all that remains of King Bodawpaya's grandiose scheme. The square ruin stands on three terraces, the walls of some of which are 48 metres (160 feet) high and pedimented and pillastered in the Pagan style. The 1838 earthquake wrought considerable damage. The roof (it never reached the stage of having its stupa) fell into the vaulted basement area where the pagoda's relics were interred. The climb is easy, notwithstanding going barefoot as one must. At the top one is rewarded with a superb view of the

Irrawaddy and the Hsinbyume Pagoda. King Bodawpaya himself is
said to have collaborated with the architect on the complicated
engineering of the building. According to Captain Hiram Cox, the
then British Resident, a series of quadrangular lead-lined pits were
prepared for the treasures, then roofed with lead tiles each 13
centimetres (five inches) square; this device was one of 'His Majesty's
own conceptions'. However, it seems that the hapless architect was
murdered lest he pass on his knowledge of the vault's design.

Mingun Bell
This bell, one of the world's largest — weighing 90 tons, over four
metres (12 feet) high and five metres (16 feet) wide at its base — was
cast by the lost wax process on Nandaw Island. It was transported
across the Irrawaddy back to the mainland on two catamarans (these
craft are now in the Sagaing Fort Museum). The bell was originally
erected on teak uprights, but these gave way during the 1838
earthquake. It seems that it was the ubiquitous Irrawaddy Flotilla
Company who re-hung it on its present steel pillars.

Hsinbyume Pagoda
This is a most attractive white pagoda which was built in 1816 by King
Bodawpaya's grandson (later King Bagyidaw) in memory of one of his
wives. Around the base are seven concentric circular terraces. The
structure itself is symbolic of Meru, the cosmic mountain, while the
undulating terraces symbolize the Seven Seas of Buddhist cosmology.
On the eastern side a staircase climbs up the centre of the terraces,
with a fine vaulted roof. This staircase was reserved for royalty, while
on either side are plain steps for lesser mortals. Around the terrace
base are niches housing *nats*, ogres and *nagas* all protecting the
pagoda. The view of the surrounding countryside from the top terrace
is stunning.

Maymyo

One of the nicest excursions from Mandalay is to drive for two and a
half to three hours — depending on the vehicle — east of Mandalay up
into the hills to the town of Maymyo. For the first half hour the drive is
through paddyfields with the blue Shan Hills ahead. Then the climb
starts. The landscape becomes wild: huge mango and acid plum trees
are interspersed with towering bamboo fronds, and with toddy palms
— bamboo ladders strapped to their trunks — awaiting harvest time.
(Toddy wine is well worth sampling.) Following a succession of

dramatic hair-pin bends the halfway point is reached; cars stop, bonnets are raised amidst much hissing of over-heated engines, and water is splashed onto tyres. As well as the usual drinks the teashops sell packets of delicious nuts and home-made crisps. Maymyo is 1,095 metres (3,510 feet) above sea level and is delightfully cool after the hot plains. Sweaters are essential for the evening.

History of Maymyo In 1886, following the exile from Mandalay of King Theebaw and the subsequent British takeover, Maymyo became an army base. Colonel May (hence Maymyo) of the Bengal Infantry led operations to quell rebel fighting in the Shan States from here. These campaigns took place over a ten-year period, long enough for the climatic advantages of Maymyo to become apparent to the British, and it grew into a popular hill station.

The Middle Fair Way

If the search for the middle way through the temples of Burma has proved elusive, some travellers may find a form of Nirvana at Maymyo Golf Club. Here the golfer's dream — that every drive comes to rest in the middle of the fairway and the rare one that disappears deep into the trees is found in a clearing with a perfect lie and sight of the green — may be fulfilled. The fairways may be rather unkempt and the greens somewhat bumpy, but you are unlikely to score better at St Andrews or Augusta.

Maymyo Golf Club is a legacy of the British, now largely enjoyed by Burmese army officers who, like their colonial predecessors, occupy the grand houses and messes surrounding the course. Whether the views across the course fill them with equal nostalgia for Surrey is uncertain, but they seem to show the same enthusiasm for golf and set off every afternoon in pursuit of the perfect score. The course is over 6,400 metres (7,000 yards), par 72 with varied and interesting holes lined by trees and interspersed with ditches and ponds.

Roger Moore (no relation but equally dashing) and I were accosted by a horde of enthusiastic young boys long before we had reached the clubhouse and were led to caddymaster U Toe Maung. We paid green fees and hired clubs and caddies at a total cost of 100 *kyats*. Having reduced the number of our supporters to three each (one to carry the clubs, one to go on ahead to locate the ball and one with general but unspecified responsibilities), the caddymaster insisted on accompanying us. At the first hole, a long tree-lined par four, my opponent hit a strong but sliced drive which disappeared into the trees on the right. My shot was similar but pulled to the left. We set off down the fairway with our entourage to find after about 230 yards a pair of boys standing beside our balls in the middle of the fairway — 'Hit a tree and bounced back, sir.'

Sights in Maymyo

The Botanical Gardens

The splendid 175-hectare (432-acre) botanical gardens were laid out by Sir Harcourt Butler, Governor of Burma. It was reclaimed from virgin marshland by Turkish prisoners of the First World War. The gardens are still beautifully maintained and seemingly all that has changed is that the bandstand has been removed. This is a perfect spot for an afternoon stroll. All manner of English 'cottage garden' seeds are for sale in charming packets marked 'Create garden to promote happiness'.

When we eventually found the green, we were offered a multiplicity of advice on the line and speed and were given five-foot puts as 'unmissable'.

We continued round the course with remarkably good scores, having miraculously avoided any trouble, until the short 13th hole where a raised tee meant that we could all see that my opponent's severely hooked shot had not rebounded onto the fairway. Leaving my ball safely on the green, we all set off into the trees and undergrowth without much hope. After a few minutes searching a cry of 'here it is' brought us back to a path (which I am certain I walked down) leading straight to the green and the ball perched up on a convenient tuft of grass allowing a full swing. My opponent gained little merit from me but took full advantage and lobbed the ball to the heart of the green to loud applause to halve the hole.

After playing 18 fine holes during which the length of our drives, the symmetry of our swings, the delicacy of our chips and the precision of our putting had all been extolled, we returned to the clubhouse. The only disappointment there was that the bar was rather short of beer (which was apparently something to do with the celebration of the centenary of the establishment of Mandalay Brewery in 1886 — the British demonstrating their priorities in building up the infrastructure after occupying Northern Burma in 1885).

Tips did not seem to be compulsory but the six new balls which we had brought with us were greatly appreciated. We were encouraged to return and if possible bring the apparently much prized possession of a gold umbrella from Lillywhites, Piccadilly (supplier of sports equipment to many generations of colonial officials). Group photographs and exchanges of addresses concluded an unscheduled but thoroughly enjoyable interlude in our Burma itinerary.

— Nigel Melville

Maymyo Town

To the south and east of the town centre stand English-style houses
each surrounded by a garden (many now used by Burmese government
officials), and an 18-hole golf course. A good way to see this area is by
bicycle, which one can hire from the Candacraig Hotel (renamed
Maymyo Guest House), itself a fine red-brick, beamed building. The
clock tower marks the centre of Maymyo: a sure sign of British
colonial town planning. The buildings here are Burmese in style but
the shop names still have a colonial ring, such as 'The Crown
Confectionery' with its regal crest. Public transport in Maymyo is by
beautifully decorated horse-drawn carriages.

Maymyo Market

From the sightseer's point of view, Maymyo has one of Burma's best
markets. The mouth-watering fruit and vegetables are laid out with
consummate style, an extra decorative touch provided by small sprigs
of flowers; in January mahonia flowers are used, their sweet smell
overpowering the pungent odour of *ngapi* (fermented fish paste). The
covered section of the market sells clothes, local fabrics and
embroidery, and has several good antique stalls. When you are
exhausted from shopping, visit the café, which specializes in milk
shakes: the avocado and strawberry ones are particularly delicious. In
finest Burmese style pots of orchids are arranged outside, while within,
each little round table has its own floral decorations. The owner, his
rigid posture recalling years of service with the British Army and
dressed in an impeccably cut dark blue coat, tells stories of days gone
by.

Pwe Kyauk and Anisakan Falls

For those with a taste for lazy days and picnics these falls are worth
visiting, though it must be admitted there is nothing particularly
distinctive about them.

Goteik Viaduct

This spectacular railway viaduct is 55 kilometres (34 miles) northeast
of Maymyo. With the government forces engaged against Shan rebels
not far to the north, this is a strategic location and is out of bounds.
However, some more adventurous travellers have been known to get
there by means of hired jeep and also, for their pains, to have been
detained for several days in the army camp near the bridge.

Pagan

Pagan's remains, scattered across a vast arid plain, positively exude antiquity and mystery. One visits individual monuments and each has its own special qualities, but it is the whole which is magnificent. Get up before daybreak and if, as Somerset Maugham did in 1930, you climb the tallest pagoda, Thatbinyu, out of the early morning mist you will see the other pagodas 'loom, huge, remote and mysterious, like the vague recollections of a fantastic dream.' Approaching midday the sun burns the colour from the landscape, leaving the red brick pagodas stark and desolate. A column of dust marks the passage of an occasional ox-cart across the dusty plain. With the declining day the colour creeps back, the trees and scrub turn from dusty grey back to lively green. The sun sets behind the hills on the far side of the Irrawaddy, filling the sky with a reddish glow.

The pagodas recall Pagan's former greatness. Once a vast and populous city, today there is but a straggling village living off sales of lacquerware and the steady trickle of tourists.

History of Pagan

The Burmese founded the Kingdom of Pagan in AD 849, but it was not until King Anawrahta ascended the throne in 1044 that Pagan entered its golden era. By 1056 Anawrahta had unified the country and had given it a national religion. From the moment that he returned from his victorious campaign against the Mons, bearing 32 copies of the Tripitaka scriptures, the building frenzy began. First he built a library, the Pitakat Taik, to house the scriptures, and then, soon after, the fine Shwesandaw Pagoda. The style of Anawrahta's early buildings was influenced by the Mon architects whom he had brought back to Pagan following his victory at Thaton. These square, squat constructions with arches and complex patterns of brickwork — temples rather than pagodas — belie the Indian origins of the faith that inspired them. Perhaps Anawrahta's most famous monument is the Shwezigon Pagoda: by the time this pagoda was started, towards the end of his 40-year reign, a distinctly Burmese style had evolved. The stark power of the earlier buildings had dissolved into softer, more fluent lines, complexity into fantasy, the golden stupa apparently weightless and ready to float up to the heavens.

Pagoda and temple building continued with unabated enthusiasm for the next two centuries. There is no record of the actual number of religious monuments built during this period, the height of Pagan's power. King Narathihapati, the last King of Pagan, allegedly tore down 10,000 buildings in order to defend his capital against an imminent Mongol invasion. At the approach of the great Khan's army in 1287, the king left the capital, earning himself the ignominious title of 'The king who ran away from the Chinese'.

From that date the city took on the role it plays today, as a monument to a Buddhist renaissance of astonishing creativity and vigour. The constant felling of trees to feed the greedy brick kilns throughout more than 230 years of construction left the hills eroded and barren. Probably by 1287 it was becoming difficult, even with the intricate irrigation systems begun by King Anawrahta, to sustain the large population. No trees, no topsoil, no rain, no food, thus no people. Pagan could not survive the harsh logic of nature.

In 1975 a fierce earthquake struck Pagan, destroying many small monuments and severely damaging some of the larger ones. Funds for restoration were made available by the United Nations, and the work was carried out to a high standard under the loving and expert eye of U Bo Kay.

Sights in Pagan

Most travellers will have only a couple of days in Pagan and must therefore be selective. If you are not travelling with a group, hire a pony cart, jeep or bicycle. If you arrive by aeroplane I suggest you go straight to the Shwezigon Pagoda in Nyaungoo near the airport, and then spend the remainder of the day around the central Pagan area. On the following day take your transport south and visit the pagodas on the way to the village of Thiripyitsaya. Most important, equip yourself with a good map; the Tourist Burma one is excellent.

The monuments in Pagan can be divided into two distinct types: temples and pagodas. Put simply, a temple is a hollow building containing one or more Buddha images. Several storeys high, the receding terraces are usually topped by a small stupa-like campanile. The large temples are the monuments to climb and get the best views of Pagan and its changing moods.

A pagoda is a solid structure, built atop several narrow terraces and usually enshrining relics of the Buddha or a particularly revered monk. For an excellent and detailed explanation of the variety of architectural styles found among Pagan's monuments, see the official *Pictorial Guide to Pagan*, on sale at all the major pagodas.

Shwezigon Pagoda

Construction of this great golden pagoda was begun by King Anawrahta and finished by his son, King Kyanzittha, in 1087. The

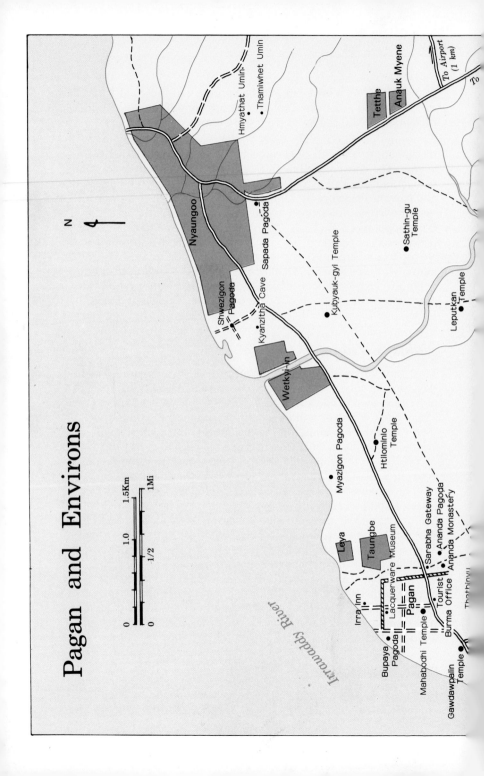

Pagan and Environs

Irrawaddy River

To Airport (1 km)
To

Anauk Myene
Tetthe

Thamiwhet Umin
Hmyathat Umin

Nyaungoo

Sapada Pagoda
Sathin-gu Temple

Shwezigon Pagoda

Kyanzitha Cave
Kubyauk-gyi Temple

Leputkan Temple

Wetkyi-in

Myazigon Pagoda

Htilominlo Temple

Leya
Taungbe

Lacquerware Museum

Sarabha Gateway
Ananda Pagoda
Tourist Burma Office
Ananda Monastery

Irra Inn

Pagan

Bupaya Pagoda

Mahabodhi Temple

Thathinyl

Gawdawpalin Temple

N

0   0.5   1.0   1.5Km

0   1/2   1Mi

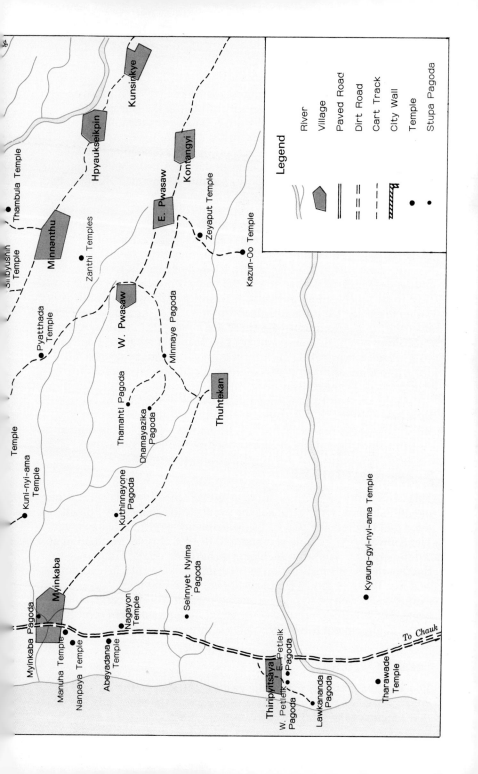

Legend

River
Village
Paved Road
Dirt Road
Cart Track
City Wall
Temple
Stupa Pagoda

Thambula Temple

Kunsinkye

Hpyaukseikpin

Minnanthu

Zanthi Temples

Sinbyushin Temple

E. Pwasaw

Kontangyi

Zeyaput Temple

Pyatthada Temple

W. Pwasaw

Kazun-Oo Temple

Kuni-nyi-ama Temple

Minmaye Pagoda

Thamahti Pagoda

Dhamayazika Pagoda

Thuhtekan

Kuthinnayone Pagoda

Myinkaba

Seinnyet Nyima Pagoda

Myinkaba Pagoda

Nagayon Temple

Manuha Temple

Nanpaya Temple

Abeyadana Temple

Kyaung-gyi-nyi-ama Temple

Thiripyitsaya

W. Petleik Pagoda   E. Petleik Pagoda

Lawkananda Pagoda

Tharawade Temple

To Chauk

Shwezigon holds a special place among Burmese pagodas for two reasons: it was the first major monument built in the Burmese (as distinct from Mon) style following the country's conversion to Theravada Buddhism, and was the first pagoda to have *nat* images allowed within its precinct — a decision that was fundamental to the rapid adoption of Theravada Buddhism during Anawrahta's reign. The Shwezigon is said to contain important relics of Gautama Buddha, two bones and the copy of a tooth.

One enters the pagoda along a covered corridor. The golden stupa rises from five terraces (three square at the base, then two round) each symbolizing a different stage of Nirvana. Around the base of the terraces are glazed plaques which illustrate the former lives of Buddha. The pioneering *nats*, 37 of them, are housed in a rather insignificant building at the northeast corner of the pagoda precinct. To reach it you have to pass a charming sideshow, a Burmese-style wishing well. A *hti* (an umbrella device normally placed on the top of the stupa) revolves in a cage, while around its base there are bowls, each marked with a wish: 'May you pass your examination', 'May you meet the one you love'. A *nat* image beside each bowl bows as the *hti* creaks around. For those intending to make a wish there is even a special counter nearby where you can change your notes into coins.

The Shwezigon Pagoda's annual festival is at the time of the November full moon. Pilgrims travel from far and wide and the pagoda and its environs are a veritable hive of activity — a splendid time to visit the Shwezigon if one is lucky enough to be in Pagan then.

Kubyauk-gyi Temple

This early 13th-century temple, near Wetkyi-in village, displays strong Indian influence. Its spire is not the usual cicada shape but straight-sided and tapered like that of the Mahabodi Pagoda in Pagan village. The Kubyauk-gyi Temple was restored in 1468. Inside are the remains of tempera wall paintings, including a charming one of Gautama Buddha during his incarnation as a hermit walking with his mother, as well as a frieze of the 28 Buddhas (24 are from previous cosmic worlds while the last four are from the present world cycle, Gautama being the 28th Buddha), each one sitting under a different tree, for each enlightenment took place under a different species.

Sarabha Gateway

The Sarabha Gateway marks the eastern entrance to the old city of Pagan. This and the small section of brick wall on either side are all that remain of the ninth-century rampart. Each side of the gate contains a niche housing Pagan's guardian *nats*, 'Mister Handsome' and his sister 'Golden Face', known collectively as 'Lords of the High Mountain'.

Ananda Pagoda and Monastery

The Ananda Pagoda was completed in 1091, soon after the Shwezigon. Of the 'four great pagodas' of Pagan, to which local folklore attributes various superlative qualities (Gawdawpalin, the most elegant; Ananda, the most beautiful; Dhammayangyi, the most massive; and That-byinnyu, the highest), Ananda holds the greatest fascination. Distinguished from the rest by its whitewash and shaped like a perfect Greek cross, it rises in graduated terraces to a height of some 52 metres (170 feet). One enters along a wooden colonnade, at the far end of which a shaft of light falls on the face and shoulders of a beautiful gold Buddha. This image, 9.5 metres (31 feet) tall, stands on a carved lotus pedestal. Around the central core of the pagoda pose three other statuesque Buddhas of similar size encircled by two concentric and lofty corridors. Lining these corridors are hundreds of tiny images housed in niches, where one can study 80 sandstone reliefs illustrating the life of the Bodhisattva from his birth to his enlightenment. The four large images represent the four Buddhas of the present world. Gautama, the most recent Buddha, was apparently placed on the western side to give him a view across the Irrawaddy to the Tan-kye Hill and Pagoda, where he had stood with his favourite disciple, Ananda, and predicted the future building and greatness of Pagan.

Retrace your steps through the great doors along the colonnade, turn left and on the left is a small red-brick building, Ananda Monastery, its walls covered in delightful frescoes depicting scenes from the Buddha's life. If you are not accompanied by a guide you will have to ask a pagoda official at the colonnade entrance to let you in and to turn on the lights. In a shed just opposite, to the left of the monastery, is a charming 11th-century standing bronze Buddha.

The January full moon marks the Ananda Pagoda festival. The approaches to the temple are crowded with stalls, pots of all shapes and sizes and rows of old black umbrellas hung like bats. Men wander around with what look to be clown-like hats which, on closer inspection, turn out to be piles of tea strainers! The place is alive with sideshows, marionettes, *nat* puppets, and even a stall where one can dress up in drag to have a picture taken. A Ferris wheel is operated by hand. A crowd of children betray the whereabouts of the cotton candy man whose pink delight is produced from a strange barrel-shaped contraption. In the evening a *pwe* is staged.

The Chindits

The successful conclusion of the remarkable Burma campaign in World War II must be largely attributed to the Chindits. By the summer of 1942 the Japanese, after taking Singapore, had advanced up through Malaya and Burma compelling the Allied forces to retreat into India. As so often in wartime the hour produced the man. 'After the disasters in Malaya and Burma,' explained John Masters, 'an unusually talented artillery officer Orde Wingate, had thought out a way to show the Japanese, and our own troops, that we could use the jungle.' A long-range penetration group known as the Chindits was formed under the controversial Wingate. The name was derived from 'Chinthe', the mythical lion which guards a pagoda entrance (a particularly fine pair sits at the foot of the Mandalay Hill). Chinthe is said to be the only 'living thing' in Burmese Buddhism which is allowed to use force.

The idea was for columns of highly trained men to pass through the Allied and the Japanese lines to attack and destroy the enemy supply lines. This sort of expedition was dependent on an excellent communications network, connecting the Chindits themselves with their supply bases in India and also with the Allied fighters and bombers. In 1943, General Wingate accompanied the British Prime Minister, Winston Churchill, to the Inter-Allied Conference in Quebec. Here Wingate spoke so eloquently on this revolutionary method of warfare that the much needed equipment 'descended on us in torrents' — including the vital air back-up. This was made up of the No. 1 Air Commando, US Army Air Corps, who boasted a number of C-47 aircraft specially adapted to snatch gliders off the ground into the air, as well as troop-carrying gliders and bombers. The ability to retrieve gliders was vital for the repatriation of the wounded.

The build-up of the Chindits to a strength of 24 battalions continued through 1943, with rigorous training at bases in India. All soldiers took a daily dose of mapacrine, which turned their faces an unhealthy yellow, to ward off the dreaded malaria.

In January 1944, with the Japanese still facing the British forces along the general line of the Indian frontier, the Chindit operation began. Some walked, others were airlifted, and in all 10,000 men and 16,000 mules — their vocal chords cut — entered Burma and infiltrated the Japanese lines. It was a bitter campaign which was to last for 20 months, and leave thousands dead on both sides. In July 1945, the 14th Army alone killed some 11,000 Japanese. Scores of Allied soldiers fell into Japanese hands whereas to the Japanese surrender was unthinkable: just six were taken prisoner in Burma. With the Chindits chiselling away at the Japanese strength from within, the conventional forces were able to make a successful three-pronged advance from India and China, achieving ultimate victory in August 1945.

Htilominlo Temple

Htilominlo is a two-storey red-brick temple built by King
Mantaungmya around 1211. On the outer walls are fragments of the
original frieze and mouldings, and around the base some glazed tiles
remain. Inside, four Buddhas face the cardinal points on both levels.
Climb up the narrow, vaulted internal staircases for a good view of
Pagan from the northeast.

Dhammayangyi Temple

Pagan's most massive temple, Dhammayangyi, was built by the wicked
King Narathu. In 1167 Narathu succeeded to the throne by smothering
first his father, King Alaungsithu, whilst asleep in his favourite temple,
Shegugyi, and then his brother, Minsthinsaw, in the Palace. Soon
thereafter he began the construction of this pagoda, no doubt to gain
some much-needed merit. The ground plan is similar to the Ananda's
but lacks its elegance, though the brickwork is fine. It is said that if on
the king's visits to the site, he was able to stick a pin between the
bricks, the mason in question would have his hands cut off prior to
being executed. Not surprisingly Narathu himself met a bloody end.
One of his queens (a Hindu princess and a former wife of his father
whom Narathu had forced into marriage) had displeased him with her
hygiene rituals and so he had had her executed. In revenge in 1170 the
princess's father sent to Narathu's court eight assassins disguised as
Brahmin priests. They quickly dispatched Narathu, and the temple was
never finished.

Shwesandaw Pagoda (Ganesha Pagoda)

Just northwest of the Dhammayangyi Pagoda stands the Shwesandaw
Pagoda. This is said to be the first monument built by King Anawrahta
after his conquest of Thaton and the Mons in 1057. Probably because
of this the pagoda displays a strong Mon influence. Each of the four
corners of the building is guarded by Ganesha, the patron saint of the
Mons. It is thought that some sacred hairs of Gautama Buddha, which
Anawrahta carried as booty from Thaton, are enshrined here. Two
square red-brick terraces lead up to three white stuccoed terraces. A
steep stairway dissects each of the terraces, and from the upper levels
there is yet another superb view of Pagan.

Shinbinthalyaung

In the same compound is a low red-brick building which contains a
long recumbent Buddha image, which is thought to date from the 11th

century. This reclining image faces east, with its head pointing south, unlike that of the Manuha Temple, which faces west with the head to the north — the traditional position of Buddha prior to entering Nirvana.

Sulamuni Temple

Just beyond Dhammayangyi stands the red-brick Sulamuni temple. It was built in 1174 by King Narapatisithu, a son of King Narathu, again no doubt as an atonement. One enters the temple precincts up a brick mounting-block, a gateway in the surrounding brick wall. The light inside is particularly striking: the sun's rays shine through the outer arches onto the central core, radiating a soft terracotta glow. The walls are decorated by murals dating from the 12th to the 19th century. All but those on the south have been badly damaged by the weather due to the vaulted openings along the outer walls. Those on the south side depict 17th-century life. On the eastern side in a recess sits a huge seated Buddha, larger than those at the other cardinal points, as the eastern entrance is reserved for royalty. The vaulted stairways to the terrace are glossy, again lit by the 'terracotta' light. The Sulamuni Temple is a favourite haunt of hawkers selling antiques; take particular care before buying any of the gems offered and in all cases bargain determinedly.

Thatbinyu Temple

The Thatbinyu Temple is a white stucco building dating from the reign of King Alaungsithu (1113−60) and, at 60 metres (200 feet), is Pagan's highest pagoda. Thatbinyu is indeed a fine building, but its main attraction is the view from its terraces, spectacular both at dawn and dusk. It is also, owing to its central position, the most popular vantage point in Pagan, which can be a disadvantage for those inclined to solitude. The Irrawaddy forms a great elbow on two sides with a strange spur of hills to the east, and into the distance the plain erupts with pagodas of all shapes and sizes and degrees of decay.

Beside Thatbinyu stands a small replica known as the 'Tally Pagoda'. For every 10,000 bricks used in the main building one went towards the 'Tally Pagoda'. The site of the 11th-century royal palace is nearby and today serves as a football pitch.

Gawdawpalin Temple

This temple, which was built during the reign of Narapatisithu

(1174–1211), is a thinner and slightly shorter version of Thatbinyu. It sustained severe damage during the 1975 earthquake, but has now been thoroughly restored.

Pagan Museum

The Pagan Museum is housed in a small, hexagonal building just across the road to the south of Gawdawpalin. It is abundantly stocked and contains some fine pieces, including small bronze 10- and 11th-century Buddha images, an 11th-century stone Buddha image of classic, simple lines, and a series of exquisitely carved small dolomite reliefs depicting the Buddha's life. However, the Museum's most prized possession is a large stone tablet, dating from 1113, inscribed in four contemporary languages, namely Pyu, Mon, Pali and Burmese. The stone was discovered in 1887 in the Kubyaukyi Temple (Myinkaba) — at the time of writing under restoration. The importance of this piece (sometimes called 'Burma's Rosetta Stone') is that it has furnished scholars with a code to the Pyu script, hitherto indecipherable.

Outside, but roofed over to shield it from the worst of the weather, is a fine sculpture collection. Here, one can compare the different styles of Burmese religious art, all of which are represented. The museum is open 9 am–4.30 pm; closed Monday.

The Road South

Myinkaba and Thiripyitsaya

Minglazedi Pagoda
Minglazedi was built by Narathihapati, 'the king who ran away from the Chinese', and was completed in 1284, just three years before Kublai Khan's invasion. As such it was the last major pagoda built in Pagan. It is noted for the glazed terracotta tiles around its terraced bases. These are apparently much prized by art thieves, which is why the pagoda is enmeshed in chicken wire.

Kupyaukgyi (Myinkaba)
This Mon-style temple was built by Prince Rajakumar, the only son of King Kyansitta, in 1113. It was not in fact until the king was in his old age that he came to know of Rajakumar's existence. The boy's mother had left court when pregnant with the gift of a valuable ring from the king. The understanding was that, if the baby was a boy, the mother should return to the court with her son and the ring, however, if the

baby was a girl, the mother should sell the ring. Many years later
Rajakumar returned with the ring. His father's delight at the discovery
of a son was tempered by the awkward fact that he had meanwhile
promised the throne to his daughter's son, Alaungsithu. Instead, the
king gave Rajakumar some land. Rajakumar was a pious man and, on
his father's death, he sold the land and built Kupyauk Gyi. The inner
sanctum is decorated with frescoes which are in the process of being
restored. Under each painting is an account, in ancient Mon script, of
the tale it depicts.

Myinkaba Pagoda
On the left as one enters into the village of Myinkaba is an inverted
bowl-like pagoda built by King Anawrahta in memory of his
predecessor and half-brother, Sokkade, whom he had killed and tossed
into a stream. It is sited beside the very watercourse down which the
victim's corpse floated on its way to the Irrawaddy.

Myinkaba Village
The most notable feature of Myinkaba village are the huge stacks of
bamboo one sees everywhere. This is the raw material for the plaited
matting which serves as the walls of houses all over Burma. Stop and
watch this intricate manufacturing operation in progress: the bamboo
is first split into strands, then deftly woven into large squares.
    The village is also famous for its traditional Mon-style lacquerware,
the secret of whose manufacture has been passed from generation to
generation since King Manuha brought his artisans with him into exile
here more than 900 years ago.

Manuha Temple
At the southern end of Myinkaba village is the Manuha Temple
complex. When in 1057 Anawrahta returned victorious to Pagan, it
was here that the captive King Manuha was brought to live. By 1059
King Manuha had built himself this two-storey square white temple
and through it conveyed a melancholy message. The three Buddhas
are uncomfortably large for their enclosures, thus illustrating his
captivity and mental stress. The facial expressions of the two seated
images are grim. That of the one reclining Buddha, on the other hand,
is smiling and serene. He faces north and is therefore on the verge of
Nirvana and release from the transitory world.

Nanpaya Temple
Beside the Manuha Temple is the charming brick-and-mud mortar
Nanpaya Temple. This was King Manuha's residence, and later

became a temple. Inside, the central plinth is empty, but on the four central pillars are beautiful stone carvings of Brahma, the Mon patron saint. The Mon people had originally been Hindu, hence the Rama goose was the emblem of the Mon Kingdom. At certain times of the day the light comes through the perforated windows, illuminating sections of the carving (but take a flashlight along). The outer walls are crenellated, and some of the sandstone friezes remain intact. A modern concrete path surrounds the temple; make sure not to leave it as the rough ground harbours some prickly briars.

Abeyadana Temple
Further south along the road on the right side is Abeyadana Temple. The legend tells us that Kyanzitta, while fleeing from his elder brother, King Sawlu, had planned to meet his lover, Abeyadana, where the temple now stands. She was late so he wandered off and fell asleep nearby. When she found him an enormous *naga* was hooded over the sleeping Kyanzitta protecting him. She screamed, waking Kyanzitta, and the *naga* was frightened away. Kyanzitta took the *naga*'s action to be a sign that he would become king. When he finally ascended the throne in 1084, he built this temple, naming it after Abeyadana, now his wife. It houses a large seated Buddha. Around the corridors are many small Buddha images in the niches, and there are also some good Mahayanist and Hindu frescoes.

Nagayon Temple
Just across the road is the Nagayon Temple. King Kyanzitta built this temple on the site where he slept protected by the *naga*. Indeed, the large Buddha image in the inner shrine is protected by a hooded *naga*. Again many of the corridor niches contain Buddha images, and part of a series of wall paintings depicting the life of Buddha decorates the entrance.

East and West Petleik Pagodas
At the entrance to Thiripyitsaya village stand the East and West Petleik Pagodas. Some 50 years ago when these 11th-century pagodas were in disrepair, it was decided to clear the debris from around their base. This operation revealed rows of unglazed terracotta tiles illustrating scenes from the Jataka, the story of Buddhas' previous lives. Sadly, many of these plaques have since either been stolen or fallen prey to the weather. As a result they are now surrounded by a rather unsightly fence and roofed over.

Lawkananda Pagoda

On the far side of Thiripyitsaya village the road comes to an abrupt end in a grove of trees. There above you, on a little hill overlooking the Irrawaddy, is the Lawkananda Pagoda. This handsome white stupa was built by King Anawrahta in 1059 and marks the southern boundary of Pagan. It is said to contain a replica of a tooth of Gautama Buddha. Poised high above the Irrawaddy, it commands excellent views to both north and south. Below it there used to be an anchorage for large trading vessels, which was used when the water level was too low for them to dock at Pagan proper.

Bupaya Pagoda

Pagan's other riverside pagoda and landmark for sailors is Bupaya Pagoda. It is about eight kilometres (five miles) upstream from the Lawkananda and just within the ancient city's northern limits. This fairy-tale pagoda sits on top of semi-circular terraces. The foundation wall rises sheer from the river's edge and is topped by a large and pleasing scallop design. It is thought that the original 'pumpkin pagoda' dated from the third century. What one sees today, however, is a recent reconstruction, the original stupa having tumbled into the river during the 1975 earthquake.

The best time to visit Bupaya is at sunset. Evening is also the time for collecting water, and from the pagoda one can watch as oxen drawing elegant carts proceed across the sandbanks and wade out into the stream, where their masters ladle water into large barrels. After the sun has dropped behind the Tan-Kye Pagoda, on the far side of the Irrawaddy, the colours intensify — red, orange, magenta; no two evenings are the same.

Mount Popa

Some 50 kilometres (30 miles) southeast of Pagan in the middle of the scorched Myingyan Plain rises up lush Mount Popa, home of the *nats*. Popa means 'flower' in Sanskrit, and Burmese legend tells that the mountain was originally the home of beautiful ogresses who played hide-and-seek on its tangled slopes. These curious characters emerged in recorded history in the form of rebels and brigands preying on travellers on their way to Pagan. It was indeed at Mount Popa that King Anawrahta amassed his army before marching on Pagan to regain his throne.

The chief mythical inhabitants of Mount Popa are a brother and sister, together known as Min Maha-giri (meaning 'Lords of the High Mountain') who are said to have lived just north of Pagan during the fourth century. Their story epitomises both the violence and essential morality inherent in *nat* beliefs. The brother bore the nickname 'Mr Handsome' and was a 'mighty blacksmith' whose hammer could cause the earth to quake. This was too much for the neighbouring king, who vowed to assassinate him. But the blacksmith was forewarned and escaped to the forest. The king then seduced Mr Handsome's beautiful sister, and made her his queen. 'I no longer fear your brother, because he is now my brother also. Invite him to Tagaung and I shall make him governor of the city.' Mr Handsome accepted the king's invitation, only to be seized, tied to a *saga* tree and burnt alive. His sister, heart-broken, leapt onto the burning pyre and perished with her brother. Only her face was not burnt, hence she became known as 'Golden Face'. The two were transformed into mischievous *nats* and lived in the *saga* tree. To avenge their murderer, they killed anything that ventured into the shade of the tree. The king felled the tree and threw it into the Irrawaddy. When the log reached Thiripyitsaya, King Thinlikyaung pulled it from the river and carved on it images of the brother and sister. With much pomp and ceremony this was transported to Mount Popa where a shrine was built and remains to this day. It is possible to stay in the monastery at the foot of the hill.

Kings of Pagan's Golden Era

Name	Relationship	Period
ANAWRAHTA	Son of Kunsaw	**1044–1077**
SAWLU	Son	**1077–1084**
KYANZITTHA	Brother	**1084–1113**
ALAUNGSITHU	Grandson	**1113–1167**
NARATHU	Son	**1167–1170**
NARATHEINKHA	Son	**1170–1173**
NARAPATISITHU	Brother	**1174–1211**
HTILOMINLO	Son	**1211–1234**
KYASWA	Son	**1234–1250**
UZANA	Son	**1250–1255**
NARATHIHAPATI	Son	**1255–1287**

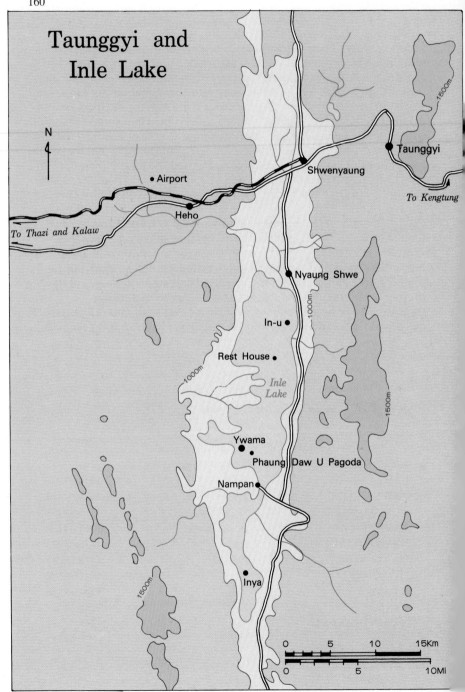

Taunggyi and Inle Lake

N

• Airport

• Taunggyi

Shwenyaung

To Kengtung

• Heho

To Thazi and Kalaw

• Nyaung Shwe

In-u •

Rest House •

Inle Lake

Ywama •

Phaung Daw U Pagoda

Nampan •

Inya •

1500m

1000m

1500m

1600m

1000m

0   5   10   15Km

0   5   10Mi

Inle Lake

The Inle Lake area is stunning, and to appreciate it properly a good two to three days is needed. Unfortunately, this is one place where the inadequacy of Burma's transport can become a distinct disadvantage. In bad weather planes do not land at nearby Heho. In such circumstances, the only way to leave the valley is a bumpy six-hour bus ride to Thazi, followed by a train journey of perhaps ten or even as much as 20 hours to Rangoon. Nevertheless the lake, the Shan capital of Taunggyi, and the magical quality of the area make the risks well worth taking.

History of the Inle Lake

The Intha people, who are of Mon rather than Shan descent, originated from the southeast of Burma around Tavoy. When or why the migration took place is unclear. Some say it was during the reign of King Narapatisithu (1173–1210). A wealth of stories surround this king. He was thought to have travelled to Tavoy on a religious mission, and there he founded a city. He is also alleged to have repulsed a vast invading Chinese army in the Inle Lake valley. Today on the bed of the lake are rows of posts, supposedly pillars of his palace. Another theory suggests that the Inthas were convicts expelled from Tavoy in the 17th century; and still another story holds that they simply became fed up with the constant battling between the Mons and the Burmese. In any event the Inthas (literally meaning 'Sons of the Lake') not only survived in their remote mountain environment, but prospered. The lake, some 32 kilometres (20 miles) long and at its widest just five kilometres (three miles) across, now has 200 settlements and a total population of some 100,000, many of whom live on floating islands of vegetation.

Sights at the Inle Lake
The Lake

Inle Lake reveals itself gradually to the approaching visitor. One advances down narrow streams hedged with high rushes, probably aboard a long canoe propelled by a lusty outboard which whisks along at terrifying speed. After several miles one emerges from this maze of waterways into a more tranquil world on a mirror of water, its glassy blue reflecting the occasional cloud. To left and right the picture is framed by serried green mountains with the centre a continuous blue.

Other than the growl of canoe buses as they whip to and fro, the silence and stillness are only disturbed by fishermen.

The fishermen of the Inle Lake have evolved an eccentric method of rowing and fishing specially suited to local conditions (the water being both shallow and very clear). By propelling their craft from the bow they can watch for approaching patches of tangled weeds and, more important, are able to see tell-tale bubbles and then pounce on the unsuspecting fish. And with only one limb engaged in providing locomotion the rest of the body is free for the business at hand: the fisherman uses his legs to push home the conical-shaped net.

Skimming along, one soon comes upon rows and rows of floating gardens bursting with an abundance of flowers and vegetables. These have been gradually built up over the years by cutting strips of dense weed from the lake floor. The tangled mass is consolidated with earth and eventually forms one of the most fertile growing media imaginable. New areas are constantly being 'grown' in shallow water: grass cuttings and weed form the foundation, then comes a layer of earth and finally top soil. When the layers of weed and earth have become integrated, strips some six feet wide and perhaps as long as a football pitch are cut loose and poled to their destinations, where they are pegged to the lake floor with long bamboo staves.

Ywama (Hairya Ywama)

The lake's largest village is Ywama, its streets a web of canals, each piece of 'land' connected by arched wooden bridges and causeways. This is a rich community, and its teak houses are generally handsome two-storeyed affairs. They are constructed on large wooden poles driven directly into the lake bed, the space below the first floor being used as a boathouse. Each dwelling has its own landing stage, often no more than a floating pavement of grass, pegged by bamboo (which doubles as mooring for visiting craft). On the plot surrounding the house are the trappings of domestic life: a tidy vegetable patch, a water pen for ducks, washing hung out to dry. At one end of the plot a small area of the canal, the size of a bath tub, is encircled by a bamboo fence; this is the scene of the family's daily washing ritual. It contains wooden planks both for sitting on as well as for use as a scrubbing board, and a large bowl for rinsing, though for the younger members a splash in the canal is preferred. From the back of the house a walkway leads to an elevated lavatory. Despite the absence of plumbing, the problem is mysteriously disposed of, and the air is purity and fragrance itself. Apparently even the dead are buried in the lake.

A pivot of social life is the morning's floating market, which

congregates on Ywama's broadest canal, alongside the village store and *nat* shrines. Here, under the protective shade of their straw *khamouts* (conical-shaped hats), chattering businesswomen manoeuvre elegant canoes filled with all manner of produce. One or two of the craft will be piled with antique boxes, pipes and so on. The Inthas' wealth is derived not only from their market gardening activities, but also from lucrative craft industries, notably weaving of Shan shoulder bags, beautiful thick Shan *longyis* as well as fine and delicate silverware. Industrial methods, however, tend towards the quaint to say the least. The blacksmith's bellows operator — his grandmother — sits perched on a small platform behind two long thick bamboo tubes, alternately pulling in and out long feather dusters, causing a very effective air draught.

Phaung Daw U

The lake is as richly endowed with pagodas and monasteries as anywhere else in Burma. In particular, the Phaung Daw U Pagoda is regarded (with the Shwedagon in Rangoon and the Shwezigon in Pagan) as one of the three principal shrines of Burma. Along the corridor leading to the pagoda are a variety of stalls, some selling Shan handicrafts, others various antiques and knick-knacks. This pagoda houses five small Buddha images, whose original forms have long since been lost under years of plastering with gold leaf by pilgrims. Once a year, at the September full moon, there is an elaborate festival during which the Buddha images are rowed around the lake to visit outlying pagodas. They are conveyed in a magnificent copy of a royal *karaweik* barge shaped like the golden swan (symbol of Buddhist royalty). The minute Buddhas sit under white royal umbrellas. Nowadays only four of the Buddhas make this regal progress. Some years ago the barge capsized wih all five aboard; their distraught guardians were only able to recover four images but, on returning to the pagoda, they found the fifth miraculously in its normal position. It has not been moved since and now guards the pagoda during the others' annual outing.

Nyaung Shwe

The village of Nyaung Shwe is the best jumping off point for a trip on the lake. It is a pleasant place to wander in; the restaurant beside the main jetty is a good place to sit, eat and watch the water traffic. The cold and wet traveller (one sometimes gets very wet on the lake) could do worse than revive his or her spirits with Mandalay rum and tea. One can also get good biscuits and bread from the local bakery.

Taunggyi

Taunggyi was founded by Sir George Scott, who was Superintendent of the Shan States around the turn of the century, as the seat of the Shan government over which he presided. It was sited 1,430 metres (4,690 feet) above sea level to provide the colonial British civil servants with a refuge from the heat. A few of the typical 'hill station' houses remain and the Taunggyi Hotel is one such. Make sure to have a flashlight in Taunggyi as there are frequent power cuts, and also a raincoat as it can be very wet. The journey from Taunggyi down to the plain and Inle Lake takes about an hour. As long as it is not raining (as it frequently is) this is a spectacular drive.

Sights in Taunggyi

Taunggyi Market
There is a market every day in Taunggyi but every fifth day it swells enormously as the regional market rotates between Taunggyi, Nyaung Shwe, Ywama, Heho and Kalaw. On these special days the market is crowded with the ethnic minorities decked out in all their finery.

Taunggyi Museum
This is an excellent small museum of ethnology and well worth a visit. There are displays showing the different ethnic groups in their costumes, models of their houses, farming methods and so on.

Kalaw

In between Taunggyi and Thazi, the junction for the Rangoon—Mandalay train, is Kalaw, another favourite hill retreat of the colonials. Many of the 'stockbroker Tudor'-style houses remain, surrounded by English gardens with an occasional overgrown tennis court. The 1,400-metre (4,600-foot) altitude makes warm clothing necessary, especially as power shortage are also frequent here and Mandalay rum is the only source of central heating. Around Kalaw live the colourful Palaung tribe (see page 53). If you are lucky enough to be in Kalaw on the regional market day you will be treated to a veritable feast of colour as the hill tribe people throng to market, buying and selling food and wares of all descriptions.

(facing page) Stone sculpture.

Pindaya Caves

A beautiful drive of some 45 kilometres (28 miles) to the northeast of Kalaw brings one to the Pindaya Caves, the home of countless Buddha images. Your flashlight will also come in handy here. A covered stairway leads to the cave entrance. Uncharacteristically there is no local legend as to why the images are there, nor indeed how long it has been thought to be an auspicious site. There are two other places of interest at Pindaya, the Shwe Ohn Hmin Pagoda and the Padah Lin Caves where archaeologists have been excavating a neolithic site. It is now possible to stay overnight at the Tourist Burma Hotel.

Traditional designs on longyis.

Other Open Places in Burma

Bassein

The most interesting way to reach Bassein is by boat (the alternative is to fly or take the train). From Rangoon one travels for 18 hours along the Twante Canal, which winds its way in and out of the Irrawaddy delta's web. With a population of 140,000, Bassein is the delta area's main town and the principal market for the surrounding 'rice bowl' of Burma. A characteristic Burmese town of wooden houses and dusty streets, Bassein is famous for its pottery and its hand-made umbrellas.

It appears that until the European traders became interested in Burma, Bassein was only a sleepy fishing village. Ralph Fitch, the English merchant chartered by Queen Elizabeth I, landed at 'Cosmin', thought to be present-day Bassein, in 1586. In the 16th century The East India Company set up a 'factory' (ie. trading post) here and at neighbouring Cape Negrais. When, in 1852, Lower Burma was annexed by the British, King Mindon pleaded unsuccessfully that he be allowed to keep the port of Bassein 'either territorially or so that he might have free and unrestrained intercourse by that port with the rest of the world,' for he 'felt as if imprisoned, landlocked in Upper Burma.' However, with the growth of the port of Rangoon and its less tortuous route to the Irrawaddy, Bassein's importance diminished.

Shwemoktaw Pagoda There are three main pagodas in Bassein, all of which are reputed to have been built by the lovers of a Moslem princess named Ohnmadani: Tazaung Pagoda, Thayaunga Yaung Pagoda and Shwemoktaw Pagoda, the most impressive of the three, which stands at the centre of the town. Every May at full moon the pagoda hosts a large festival. A large majority of the festival stalls sell pots, reflecting Bassein's major industry. Continuing the town's entrepreneurial traditions, many of the stall-holders at festivals up and down the country are from the Bassein area.

Twante

It is possible either to stop off at Twante for a day on the way to Bassein or to take a day boat trip along the Canal from Rangoon. The journey is more interesting than the destination, a nice quiet town whose inhabitants specialize in pottery. Bassein and Twante are 'open' to visitors. However, if Tourist Burma does not have someone available to accompany you, obstacles are likely to emerge. With any of these 'brown area' destinations chances of success are much higher out of the peak tourist season.

Sandoway

A mere 25-minute hop by air from Rangoon and you are at one of the world's most beautiful beaches — miles and miles of silver sand lapped by the Bay of Bengal with little villages clustered under the shade of the palm trees. Early morning sees the fishermen set out or return from an overnight trip while the women spread out small fish to dry on bamboo mats: some are even tucked into their hats. At sundown the dried fish are transferred into baskets and carried home along the soft sands, coloured pink by the setting sun. These crystal-clear waters are a snorkeller's paradise.

The village of Sandoway is a charming spot, with the usual market and teashops, several of which serve delicious food. It also boasts a nine-hole golf course. The village is used as a resort by top Burmese officials and foreign diplomats, whose tasteful villas stand along the waterfront. The Ngapali beach, where there is a fairly spartan branch of Rangoon's Strand Hotel, is just down the coast from Sandoway Village.

Shin Aung Village

Those who plan to spend several days in Sandoway should hire a jeep and explore the hinterland. A few miles inland and you are in the foothills of the Arakan Yomas. This is elephant country, where the animals work in the teak forests. Shin Aung village is one of the many in the area where elephants are trained. An elephant costs roughly 90,000 *kyats*. Most are leased to the government. A one-year contract earns the owner 30,000 *kyats*. While the men work the elephants and till the land (though according to ancient tradition women plant rice, since 'rice is grown for the gods'), the women spin and weave. On the terrace of a house one may see an old lady spinning, and underneath in the shed alongside the cows her daughter sits on the earthen floor weaving. This is a Chin village, so they specialize in thick cotton *longyis* similar to blankets, often coloured white.

Prome

North of Rangoon on the eastern banks of the Irrawaddy is Prome. Just a few miles northeast of the town is Srikshetra, one of Burma's most interesting early archaeological sites. As the Pyu people moved south from their Tibetan homeland around the first century AD, they are thought to have settled beside the Irrawaddy's busiest ports. To visit Prome and Srikshetra one can either hire a jeep from Rangoon (a drive of about four to five hours), take the train from Rangoon or sail

by boat downstream from Pagan.

Excavations at Srikshetra show that a wall enclosed three sides of the city, the sea the fourth. Three cone-shaped pagodas formed a triangle outside the city wall. These extraordinary buildings, which still stand, were used as lookout towers and fortresses to guard the city. Incorporated within the city walls were more watchtowers, only accessible by drawbridge from inside the city. On the three landward sides of the city was a broad moat. Parts of the palace site and moat have been excavated. The Pyu capital remained at Srikshetra until the eighth century when it was moved north to Halin. The Pyu dynasty foundered around the mid-ninth century and Srikshetra itself was finally destroyed by the Burmese King Anawrahta in 1057 on his return from Thaton and his conquest of the Mons.

Sights in Prome

Srikshetra Museum
Beside the small railway station of Hmawza — a delightful place reminiscent of an English rural station, complete with beds of flowers on the platform — is a museum. It is often locked, as the curator doubles as headmaster of the local school. The museum contains some interesting pieces excavated from the palace, including a Pyu-dynasty *thanaka-kyauk-pyin*. This is a stone on which the *thanaka* bark was ground to make the cosmetic powder. Many of the better pieces, however, are now in the Rangoon Museum. Take a walk in the immediate vicinity of the museum and discover small pagodas hidden away, wooden monasteries shaded by great jacaranda and flame-of-the-forest trees.

Payamna, Payagyi and Bawbawgyi Pagodas
These extraordinary shaped, vast pagodas erupt out of the flat Prome landscape to form a triangle of defence around the city wall; for in addition to their religious functions they served as watchtowers. They are thought to have been constructed around the fifth century: in their heyday they would probably have been plastered and painted, but their red brick is now decorated with an assortment of vegetation. A tiny *hti* balances on the top of each one and there are no discernible entrances, which makes it hard to work out how they could have been used as watchtowers.

Bebe Pagoda
Near the Bawbawgyi stands the Bebe Pagoda, another strange-looking construction, cube-shaped with an inverted begging bowl forming a hat

on top. This pagoda is thought also to date from the fifth century.

Shwesandaw Pagoda

Gautama Buddha is alleged to have preached a sermon on the site of the Shwesandaw, hence it ranks among Burma's most famed pagodas. The origins of the building are not clear. One version claims that the pagoda was first built by two merchant brothers soon after the Buddha's visit, then some 100 years later it was rebuilt by the 'national hero king', Dwut-Tabaung, to enshrine a hair of the Buddha. What is certain, however, is that the pagoda has been damaged several times by earthquakes. Today it stands, a beautiful gold stupa on a base of square terraces.

The Irrawaddy at Prome

At Prome, the Irrawaddy is wide, stately and busy. Some of Burma's newly developed oilfields are in the Prome district, and many of the ships in port are extraordinary-looking oil transport vessels. At Toungoo, 'as the crow flies' some 130 kilometres (80 miles) east of Prome, is one of Burma's largest sawmills. 'Villages' of teak rafts (each one has its own little house for its pilot) are moored around the port awaiting transport to the sawmills. Burma's forests account for approximately 76% of the world's supply of teak. An estimated 4,000 elephants are used for extraction and haulage. Along the sandy banks around Prome's port — hardly a crane and no suspicion of a container in sight — camp the families of the extra labour associated with the timber trade. Many of these are Chins and Kachins from the north who, in the cool of the early morning, are to be seen wrapped in their traditional thick cotton blankets. The mountainous river bank to the west is dotted with pagodas. One can visit the two most revered, Hsin De and Shwe Bontha, as ferries ply the river throughout the day.

Off the Beaten Track

Myohaung and the West

The Arakan is a magical region. Officially it is out of bounds to
visitors, but Tourist Burma nevertheless labels it as open. In effect this
means that if there are no border troubles or, more important, if a
guide is available to accompany you (there are none resident in the
Arakan), you may be given permission to go. You can either fly direct
to Akyab, the jumping-off point for visiting the ancient capitals around
Myohaung, or stop off *en route* for a lazy day or so at the beach resort
of Sandoway (see page 169).

History of the Myohaung Area This part of the Arakan is rich in
archaeological remains. There were four Arakanese dynasties. The last
dynasty, the Mrauk-U, which lasted from the 14th to the 18th century,
was Arakan's golden age. During the 15th century Mrauk-U grew into
an extremely rich city state, based mainly on its abundant rice
production. With an annual rainfall of around 650 centimentres (250
inches) harvests never failed, while her Indian neighbours suffered
severe droughts. So Mrauk-U was fortunate to have a ready-made
market for her surplus rice. It was during the 1660s that Father
Manrique, the Portuguese Jesuit, lived for two years at the court of the
dynasty's most famed king, Thiri-thu-dhamma, and left us with a
detailed and intimate narrative of palace life and intrigue. Arakan's
demise began in 1666 when the Mogul emperor Auranzebe invaded
Chittagong, then a part of the Arakanese empire. The loss of
Chittagong was followed by a series of civil disturbances inside the
Arakan proper. Constant rebellions and assassinations continued
through the 17th and 18th centuries. Between 1666 and 1710 there
were ten kings. In 1784 the Burmese king, Bodawpaya, finally took
advantage of the Arakan's weakness and invaded, bringing the Mrauk-
U dynasty to an end.

Akyab

Akyab, the capital of Arakan State, stands on a small island at the tip
of a spit of land jutting into the Bay of Bengal. It was built by the
British after the annexation of Arakan in 1826 as their administrative
headquarters. The site was chosen both for strategic and health
reasons: it guards the mouths of the Kaladan and Magu Rivers, and
the sea breeze was thought to stave off the ever-present threat of
cholera. Visitors are normally put up in a charming Tudor-style Circuit
House, so one's fellow guests tend to be government officials on tours

of inspection. One can either eat out — Akyab boasts excellent *mohingha* shops for breakfast and, with its large Muslim community, several good vegetarian restaurants — or you can order your meals to be brought in. The latter will arrive in a tiffin box. Akyab makes up for its lack of important sights with an abundance of charm: wooden monasteries, mosques, grand houses left over from the colonial days and, dominating the town, a fine Queen Victoria Jubilee Clock. A leisurely stroll from the Circuit House is the wind-swept promontory of Akyab. To the west are views over the Bay of Bengal, to the east the town itself and the mouth of the Kaladan River. All kinds of craft, many looking totally unseaworthy, grapple with nets and lines. At the point where the currents meet they have to drop anchor before tacking up the east coast.

Myohaung

The only way to reach Myohaung is by boat. The government boats wend their way upstream, first on the Kaladan and then the Lemro River. Little boats abound, some piled high with pots and miscellaneous wares. In the wider stretches of water strange, triangular nets suddenly rise from the water. How the fish are stopped from escaping before the fisherman ceases grappling with the pulleys is a mystery. Away from the coast palms are replaced by great spreading trees, their gnarled roots often reaching into the river. As always in Burma, hills frame the horizon. Arrival at the halfway stop is heralded by the sight of an enormous pagoda high on a hill guarding all around. One's vessel nips down a side canal to reach the village. Here you can disembark, have a drink, and buy the locally-grown nuts or beans baked and salted to a perfection of crunchiness. At each stop more and more people crowd on, so not only the two decks but also the roof are filled to capacity. There are likely to be soldiers on board *en route* to take up border duties; occasionally a particularly enthusiastic marksman will load his rifle and take a pot-shot at a passing bird! To approach Myohaung the river steamer turns from the wide Lemro River and picks its way up a small creek, manoeuvring between many small craft and the huge trees that arch over the water. Green hills crowned with pagodas dominate the middle distance.

Myohaung, like Akyab, has no hotel but instead a charming wooden Circuit House. The plumbing consists of an inside washroom with an enormous stone trough of water, the substitute shower head is an aluminium bowl, while outside wooden cubicles house 'thunder boxes'. Present-day Myohaung is a busy market town with the usual collection of monasteries, brown wooden and mat houses and just two cars, both of which belong to the Town Council.

Sights in the Myohaung Area

Old Mrauk-U City

Just behind the Circuit House stand the crumbling walls of outer
Mrauk-U. As at the Forbidden City in Beijing, the king's palace was
an inner city forming the core of Mrauk-U. The city walls did not run
in a continuous line but merely filled in the gaps between natural
barriers of mountains and tidal rivers. A line of artificial lakes was
constructed on the eastern city boundary, the most vulnerable to
Burmese attack. In fact, it is said that in the 14th century a Burmese
invasion was quelled by the opening of the sluice gates. As so often in
Burma nothing remains of the palace, which was built of teak. Father
Manrique tells us it was lacquered and 'ornamented with carvings and
gilt mouldings'. However, within the city walls the plain is dotted with
pagodas, some so long forgotten that they are now little more than
overgrown mounds, although a few still stand intact. The old library is
a fine building. Very near the Circuit House, but still within the wall,
the Department of Archaeology has set up a little field museum, which
contains some beautiful pieces found here and at Vesali.

Shittaung Pagoda

The Shittaung Pagoda is a curious building looking more like a huge
grey stone wedding cake than a pagoda. Built in 1535 by King Min Bu,
the Shittaung, or '8,000 Pagoda' (so named on account of the many
images it contains) stands in the northwest corner of the outer city. It
was built by Indian workmen brought back by King Min Bu from
eastern Bengal following a victorious campaign which saw the
annexation of Chittagong. One approaches up a long staircase and
enters through the great eastern door which still has its original stone
hinges. No mortar was used in the construction, but instead the bricks
were fitted together like a jigsaw puzzle, then at regular intervals held
in place by stone brackets. Inside are two concentric passages, the
outer one decorated with a frieze of Arakanese musicians and the
inner one by scenes from 550 stories of the Buddha's life. At the centre
stands a 14th-century Buddha image carved from a single piece of
stone, beautiful in its simplicity. As one walks along the cool outer
passage, the occasional arch allows a view through to the inner
sanctum. To the west is the coronation and meditation hall, where
King Thirithu-Dhamma was crowned on 23 January 1635. During
World War II the Japanese used this massive pagoda as an ammunition
dump.

Andaw Pagoda

King Min Bin also built the Andaw Pagoda, the architecture of which is of a style similar to that of Shittaung — a square grey building surrounded by nine small stupas and Buddha images and topped by a solid dome. Again no mortar was used. The inside plan is similar. Andaw is said to have a wisdom tooth of Gautama Buddha enshrined in the inner sanctum.

Htukkan Thein Pagoda

The literal translation of Htukkan Thein is 'lifting up heavy slabs of rock by using wooden levers', which is presumably how this and the other massive grey pagodas were built. Htukkan was an ordination hall, and the niches in the inside corridor contain some fine stone Buddhas interspersed with carvings of 64 contemporary Arakanese hairstyles. Originally these carvings would have been painted and on some the *longyi* pattern is still discernible. An hour or so before sunset is the best time to visit this pagoda. Shafts of evening sun are channelled through the arches and illuminate the Buddha images.

Around Myohaung

The countryside around Myohaung is filled with fascinating sights. Drive past the old Mrauk-U city gate (the White Elephant Gate) into a vast plain surrounded by mountains. On top of one of the foothills in the village of Nagyan stands a monastery, once a centre for insurgents. From here there is a marvellous view of the Lemro River. Visit Laung Yet city (the last centre of the Four City States dynasty, 11th to 14th centuries), which is said to have housed 8,000 pagodas. Although most have disappeared several survive in good condition and are worthy of a visit, in particular Laymyathna Pagoda, Lanr Pan Prauk Pagoda and Radanamanaung Pagoda, which was recently given a new grey dome.

Vesali

The most interesting of the old cities is Vesali (third to tenth centuries), which has been excavated by Burma's archaeological department. The fort, with an outer wall two-and-a-half metres (eight feet) thick, is an impressive sight. It has been excavated into neat squares which expose the fine red brickwork. In peace-time it was used as an assembly and audience hall, the palace being nearby. The palace itself remains unexcavated as a village presently occupies the site. A short walk away, on Thanya Yadana Hill, stands a pagoda and monastery, where the Second Buddhist Synod was reputedly held not long after the Buddha's death.

Singuttara Hill

Perhaps the Arakan's most fascinating sight is the fabled Singuttara Hill, which lies a day's river journey from Myohaung. It was the original home of the Mahamuni Image (now in Mandalay) and is still the home of the Yattara Bell. Its fascination lies not so much in its visual appeal as in the fact that the ownership of these two relics figured prominently in Arakan's history. It was believed that the Mahamuni Image, one of the five known actual likenesses of Gautama Buddha, was cast by a heavenly sculptor, the Lord of Paradise, while the Lord Buddha rested on Singuttara Hill after a week's preaching. So the Arakanese found themselves guardians of the oldest, most mysterious and most holy object of the Buddhist world. There is some scientific evidence to support the claim that an image has stood here since the time of Buddha. Singuttara Hill stands within the ancient city of Dhannavadi, whose walls are still traceable, and are said to date prior to the first century AD. The same antiquity is claimed for the remains of the original pagoda which housed the image. Magic was used to guard the image, it being held that its destruction or removal would herald the fall of the kingdom. On the Yattara Bell, which rests beside where the image once stood, are inscribed magical ciphers used to put invaders to flight by deranging their astrological chart and so placing them in jeopardy. Even the powerful Burmese King Bodawpaya took the precaution of employing experts to tamper with the ciphers before making his successful odyssey to secure the Mahamuni Image. Today the hill has a mournful, deserted air. The bell is still there and there is a pagoda built much later, in the Pagan style — the original was destroyed by the Mongols in AD 957.

The remainder of Burma's west, including the Chin Hills and the upper reaches of the Chindwin River, are truly out of bounds, though it has been known for adventurous hikers to take surreptitiously to the hills.

Moulmein and the South

Moulmein is another 'brown area' destination, more often than not 'off limits' depending on the availability of a Tourist Burma guide and the activities of the smugglers on the Thai—Burmese border. A large proportion of black-market goods travel from Thailand over the Three Pagodas Pass, thence by rail through Moulmein, Thaton and into central Burma. The contraband is merely thrown out of the window at pre-determined locations. However, these activities cause the authorities to feel that the trains can sometimes be a security risk.

For second-time visitors to Burma, a trip to Moulmein is well worth the effort. Travel to Pegu by road or rail then on via Kyaik-Tyo with its golden pagoda perched on top of a gilded boulder (see page 100). Continue south through Thaton, the former capital of the Mon Kingdom and an early centre of learning (old Thaton has long since disappeared, but there are several interesting sights in and around the present-day city). Then on to Moulmein, further still to Amherst and eventually, if you are very lucky, to Mergui.

Moulmein

Moulmein itself is a charming city, built at the mouth of the wide Salween River and the confluence of four smaller rivers, with the Moulmein Hill behind. The west of the city is protected from the Gulf of Martaban by Bilugyun Island but nonetheless, Moulmein has the feeling of a seaside town. Until the close of the first Anglo-Burmese war Moulmein was a small trading post famous for pearl-fishing and teak, which was floated down the mighty Salween River. With the signing of the Treaty of Yandabo in 1828, the Province of Tenasserim (including Moulmein) was ceded to the British. Between then and the end of the second Anglo-Burmese war in 1852 (and with it the cession of the whole of Lower Burma) Moulmein was the centre of the colonial administration.

The wooden houses are often painted in pastel colours, and the iron balconies covered in flowering potted plants. A gentle sea breeze rustles in the palm trees. The atmosphere — perhaps something to do with the smuggling — is exciting and carefree. The town's traffic mainly consists of *tongas* and vintage cars, though recently a few modern (smuggled) vehicles have appeared.

The Strand and the Market
An evening stroll on the Strand is an exercise in nostalgia. This is a 19th-century promenade along the waterfront, probably constructed during Moulmein's British period between the first and second Anglo-Burmese wars. It is lined with rather smart stucco houses and the occasional café and restaurant, where one can sit outside and watch the world pass by. Moulmein has wonderful prawns and other seafood. At the northern end of the Strand is the market. The fishermen tie up their boats and unload their catch directly onto the stalls. Another large section of the market is given over to fresh flowers.

Kyaikthanlan Pagoda
Rudyard Kipling made a two-day stop at Moulmein in 1889. Ever since there has been speculation regarding the identity of the pagoda in his

famous lines:

> By the old Moulmein pagoda,
> Lookin' lazily at the sea,
> There's a Burma girl a-sitten'
> And I know she thinks of me.

The most likely candidate seems to be Kyaikthanlan, a gilded pagoda set in the hills with wide terraces from which there are fine views over the city and harbour. One of the out-buildings houses the Thihar Thanna Throne, a beautiful gilded piece inlaid with glass on which Buddha's tooth was carried from Kandy in Ceylon during King Mindon's reign. Near the pagoda is the Yadanar Bon-Myint Monastery, a huge wooden building constructed by one of King Mindon's wives who became a nun after his death.

Other Religious Sites

There is an abundance of religious monuments in and around Moulmein, the most notable being Uzena Pagoda with its figures of the Buddha in the different stages before attaining enlightenment, the cave of 10,000 Buddhas (Kawgaun) and the Hapayon Cave. But if your time is limited, I suggest a trip by one of the small craft you can hire in the harbour to Gaung-Se Kyun ('Head-Washing Island'). It was water from this island which was used for the ceremonial head-washing of the king during the Buddhist New Year celebrations. The island sits at the confluence of five rivers. On it there is a monastery surrounded by stupas and an enormous statue of Buddha looking back across the water to Moulmein and the Kyaikthanlan Pagoda. As you approach the Gaung-Se Kyun its thin white stupas sparkle against the green trees and the island seems to hover just above the water, giving rise to the belief that it was suspended from the heavens by a silken thread and that its surrounding water was sacred.

Amherst

The town of Amherst, once a British coastal resort, is about 90 kilometres (55 miles) south of Moulmein. It is sometimes declared 'out of bounds' owing to the activities of smugglers or rebels. But if possible hire a jeep and make a day trip. The main pagoda in Amherst, though of no particular architectural merit, enjoys an outstanding location, perched on rocks lapped by the sea and joined to the land by a covered causeway which floods at high tide. Beside the causeway is a huge stone boat, apparently built by a retired British naval officer in the 1930s in which to live out his years of leisure.

The Judson Memorial A few miles from the pagoda is the grave of Anne Judson, wife of Adoniram Judson, a Baptist and the first American missionary in the Far East. They arrived in Burma in 1813. Beside the grave is a memorial stone to their lives. Mr Judson compiled the first English-Burmese dictionary.

Setse Beach

Before starting the hot return journey to Moulmein, pause at Setse Beach for a refreshing swim in the clear waters of the Gulf of Martaban. Miles and miles of white sand, once a favourite playground of colonialists, are today deserted save for the occasional fisherman or coral diver.

Thanbyuzayat Cemetery

Further north is the enormous war cemetery at Thanbyuzayat. Most of those buried here lost their lives working as Japanese prisoners of war on the Burma–Siam railway, the famous line that crosses the Bridge on the River Kwai in Thailand. The cemetery, immaculately kept by the Commonwealth War Graves Commission, is a garden filled with small crosses and grave markers with name, rank and age of the deceased, its beauty and calm rendering it the more poignant.

Mudon

Just before Mudon, the last stop before arriving back in Moulmein, fantastic rock outcrops suddenly erupt out of the paddy-fields. One such, topped by a pagoda, is named Moulmein Popa, after Mount Popa, home of the *nats*, near Pagan. The picturesque Kandawlay and Kandawgyi Lakes beside the town of Mudon provide an ideal excuse for a tea stop and a leg stretch. The first lake is for the ladies to bathe in, the second for the men. On the far side of the lakes stand two white pagodas.

Vicarious Visits

One of the frustrating things about Burma is the vast number of fascinating places one is not allowed to visit for security reasons. Out-of-bound locations in southeast Burma include Tavoy, Mergui, Tenasserim and the Mergui Archipelago. One can, however, imbibe their atmosphere through the pages of Maurice Collis's magnificent book *Siamese White*, based on the life of the 17th-century adventurer

and trader, Samuel White, of Bath, who became virtual king of Mergui. Collis himself served as the British Resident in Mergui during the 1930s and developed an intimate knowledge of the area.

The East: Kayah, Karen and Shan States

All of the Kayah State, most of the Karen and the majority of the Shan States are truly out of bounds to the traveller. These are the areas where the Burmese authorities have been fighting protracted wars with armies of the minority peoples. At Burma's independence in 1947, the Karens, Shans and the other major ethnic minorities were persuaded to join the Union of Burma on the basis that the new Constitution gave them the option of their own independence. However, independence was not forthcoming and several minorities have been fighting for their autonomy ever since. The pattern of fighting seems to be that the government forces advance during the dry season, and then minority armies consolidate and regain their position during the wet season. One of the most formidable forces is the 10,000-strong National Liberation Army of the largely Christian Karen people. According to a senior military attaché in Bangkok, 'The Karens are the best guerilla fighters in Southeast Asia and among the best in the world. They are led by officers schooled in the British tradition and are highly disciplined and deeply motivated by nationalism.' Indeed their general, Bo Mya, served with the Chindits during World War II, and their professionalism has attracted foreigners to fight alongside them for no pay. Their funds are very limited as, unlike some of the other armies, they refuse either to grow or trade in opium. Their revenues come from the border tax of 5 percent which they levy on smugglers going to and coming from Thailand.

Kaya State is Burma's smallest and does not have an army of its own. It is on the fringes of Karen territory, and its people are called Red Karens, not for their politics but for their preference for red clothing. The capital of Kayah is Loikaw, where the Padaung tribe and their 'giraffe women' live (see page 53).

A small slice of the Shan States around the beautiful Inle Lake (see page 161) is open to tourists but in much of the remainder of this extensive area of mountain and jungle the government is fighting the Shan rebels and the opium-growing warlords who finance many of the minority armies. The legendary Khun Sa, head of the Shan United Army, is said to be the supreme warlord of Golden Triangle drug operations, moving his headquarters back and forth across the border depending on the activities of the Burmese and Thai military. Khun Sa himself denies trafficking in narcotics and depicts himself as a freedom fighter trying to win autonomy from Rangoon for Burma's two million Shans.

The North: Mogok and Kachin

The north is another fascinating part of Burma but sadly also closed to the visitor. Again security is the reason. Here, as well as in the northern Shan States, the government is fighting the remnants of the Kuomintang Third and Fifth Armies, which were originally enlisted by the Burmese in the 1950s in their crusade against encroaching communism. In return for the exiles' help, a blind eye was turned to their lucrative opium-growing activities. Now several decades later the communist threat has receded and the Burmese government finds itself in the costly and difficult business of trying to eradicate the drug trade.

If by some miracle you get permission to visit the north, a sensible route would be to travel by train from Mandalay to Myitkyina, Burma's largest northern town, and then return to Mandalay by boat down the Irrawaddy. During the dry season the low water may make the Myitkyina to Bhamo section impassable; if so you could travel that part by jeep. It is by all accounts a beautiful stretch of jungle road.

The Road to Myitkyina

Some 100 kilometers (60 miles) north of Mandalay the train passes through **Shwebo**. The great King Alaungpaya, 'a mere village headman', was born here and it was from Shwebo that he led his victorious forces against the Mons. For a brief five years, from 1755 to 1760, he made Shwebo his capital. This founder of the third and last Burmese empire is buried in his birth place, where his headstone still stands.

Mogaung, 100 kilometres (60 miles) south of Myitkyina, is the centre of Burma's jade mining region. The jade mined in this area has always been much sought after by the Chinese. It is high quality jadeite, as opposed to the less valuable Chinese nephrite. The mining methods are still primitive, including 'fishing for jade', whereby the miner paddles barefoot, feeling for the jade with his toes.

The railway runs up the western shores of the Irrawaddy with **Myitkyina** being the northern terminus. The town stands on a 'scorching' plain at the entrance to the narrow Hukawng Valley, most 'fateful of all the ways of entry into Burma'. It was from Myitkyina along this valley (past the amber mines) that in the summer of 1942 thousands of refugees fled before the advancing Japanese. The monsoon rains arrived early that year and some 20,000 people died from malaria on this journey. Today Myitkyina is a typical sleepy Burmese market town. If the Ledo Road had ever fulfilled its purpose (see page 39) it would instead have become a major entrepot for goods traded between India and China. Above Myitkyina the upper reaches of the Irrawaddy are a multitude of streams and riverlets. Just north of the town the Irrawaddy makes a boisterous emergence from the foothills and then spreads out and adopts the calm, noble personality that it will maintain for most of its 1,600-kilometre (1,000-mile) journey to the coast. There are, however, stretches south of Bhamo where the river banks become steep cliffs and the river bottom drops away to extreme depths. According to local legend these waters are inhabited by monsters (and no doubt by *nats*). The boat trip from Bhamo to Mandalay should take three days, but it has been known for boats to get stuck on sandbanks for several days.

A stop at **Mogok**, some 115 kilometres (70 miles) northeast of Mandalay, and its gem mines would be fascinating. This is even more difficult to arrange as the authorities have a major gem-smuggling problem to contend with and are apparently wary of inquisitive foreign eyes. Rubies are Mogok's most prized gems, though sapphires, emeralds and lapis lazuli are among the other precious stones mined in the area. (If you are a gem merchant, the easiest place to see Burma's gems is at the International Gem Emporium which is held in Rangoon every year.) From Mogok it would be possible to rejoin an Irrawaddy boat but it may be easier to continue south to Mandalay by road.

Glossary

chinthe	mythical lion who guards a pagoda entrance
daw	title of respect for an older woman
hti	golden umbrella at the summit of a pagoda
karma	a person's fate due to his actions in a previous incarnation
kyaung	Buddhist monastery
lapet	pickled tea
longyi	sarong worn by both sexes
eingyi	blouse worn with the *longyi*
mohingha	Burmese breakfast of noodles and soup
nat	a spirit
ngapi	paste made from fermented prawns
nirvana	the state of perfect enlightenment, of release from the cycle of birth, suffering and death
pwe	an entertainment
pyongyi	Buddhist monk
shin-pyu	initiation ceremony into the monkhood for boys
shwe	gold, golden
thanaka	tree whose bark is ground into a cosmetic
U	title of respect for an older man
viss	unit of measure, equal to approximately 1.6 kilograms or 3.5 pounds
ponna	Brahman astrologer
mudra	the different hand positions of the Buddha portrayed in works of art
Tripitaka	Buddhist scriptures

Transliteration from the Burmese does not conform to a single system; one comes across the same word spelled a multitude of different ways. For the avoidance of confusion we have tried to be consistent in the spelling.

Major Festivals

March/April (Tagu) Tagu is the month when Thingyau, the Water Festival, is celebrated. It marks the visit to earth of Thagyamin, King of the *Nats*, and the start of the Burmese New Year.

April/May (Kason) At the full moon the birth, enlightenment and attainment of Nirvana of Gautama Buddha is celebrated.

June/July (Waso) The full moon heralds the start of the three-month Buddhist Lent.

August/September (Tawthalin) This is the month of boat races, including the lavish festival on Inle Lake.

September/October (Thadingyut) The full moon of Thadingyut marks the end of Buddhist Lent and Gautama Buddha's return to earth. His return is celebrated by the Festival of Lights. For three days Burma is illuminated by millions of candles and lamps and a festive air prevails.

October/November (Tazaungmon) During Tazaungmon the Weaving Festival is held. Throughout the night of the full moon the clack-clack from the looms of unmarried girls reverberates around pagoda precincts. They are competing to weave new robes for the monks. If in Burma during this festival, try and visit the Shwedagon Pagoda where the beauty and romance of this scene is paramount.

November/December (Nadaw) Nadaw is the month of *nat* festivals.

December/January (Pyatho) During Pyatho the majority of local pagoda festivals are celebrated.

January/February (Tabodwe) Tabodwe is the time of the Harvest Festival (Htamane).

Recommended Reading

Many of the empire builders and adventurers, priests and merchants, and other motley travellers that Burma has attracted have written about the country, often with style, perception and, not infrequently, wit.

As in the case of India, colonialists (disciplined, enquiring, keen-eyed types) have provided some of the most useful as well as enjoyable accounts. Two such were Sir Henry Yule and Sir George Scott — both quintessential men of the Victorian Raj. Yule, who joined the Bengal Engineers in 1840, travelled to Burma as secretary to Colonel Arthur Phayre's Mission to Ava in 1855. His 380-page *A Narrative of the Mission to the Court of Ava in 1855* (Smith, Elder, and Company 1858; Oxford in Asia Historical Reprints, Oxford University Press 1968) both chronicles the mission voyage up the Irrawaddy to the court of King Mindon and also provides a penetrating social study. The facsimile edition has an informative introduction by Professor Hugh Tinker. The copious and often beautiful illustrations include drawings and watercolours by the mission's official artist, Colesworthy Grant, as well as by the author, helpful maps and photographs by Linneus Tripe — a positive cornucopia of a book.

Sir George Scott joined the Burma commission in 1886 and proceeded to build an immensely distinguished career, notably as Superintendent for the Northern and later Southern Shan States. He wrote prolifically and with great insight and sensitivity about the country and its people. In particular, *The Burman, His Life and Notions* (Macmillan and Sons 1910) and *Burma as it was, as it is and it will be* (George Redway 1886) remain, with minor exceptions, accurate descriptions of daily life, a century after they were written.

In the late 19th century, the ship on which Rudyard Kipling was travelling made a brief stop in Rangoon and then in Moulmein. He records this short interlude in Volume 1 of *From Sea to Sea* (Doubleday McClure, New York 1899 and Macmillan, London 1900). In these few days he managed to imbibe the feeling and beauty of the country and its occupants. Burma also features in several of his poems and the much quoted 'Mandalay' is most conveniently found in the *Oxford Dictionary of Quotations* (Oxford University Press, Third Edition 1979). Another brief but perceptive visitor was Somerset Maugham. He describes his voyage up the Irrawaddy in *Two Gentlemen in the Parlour* (Heinemann 1936). Two more modern travellers have written lively accounts of their Burmese adventures; *Golden Earth* by Norman Lewis (reprinted 1984, Eland Books, London and Hippocrene Books, New York) and *The Great Railway*

Bazaar: by Train Through Asia by Paul Theroux (Random House 1975).

The historian and novelist, Maurice Collis, had in the 1920s been a member of the Indian Civil Service stationed near Mandalay in Sagaing and later in Rangoon. His *Land of the Great Image* (Faber 1942) tells the remarkable tale of the Portuguese Jesuit Manrique's journey to, and three years' sojourn at, the Arakan capital of Myohaung in the 1620s. Of his many other books on Burma, *Siamese White* (Faber 1951, and D D Books, Bangkok 1982) and *Trials in Burma* (Faber) are the most interesting.

George Orwell was another English novelist who found himself stationed in Burma in the 1920s. He portrays the stilted Raj life in *Burmese Days* (Penguin 1982) with acid disdain. His subsequent short stories on Burma, 'A Hanging' in *Decline of the English Murder* (Penguin 1983) and 'Shooting an Elephant' in *Inside the Whale* (Penguin 1982), are particularly moving.

Perhaps the best English novel set in Burma is F Tennyson-Jesse's *The Lacquer Lady* (reprint, Virago 1979), a beautifully written and spellbinding reconstruction of the extraordinary true story of Fanny Moroni at the court of King Theebaw and Queen Supayalat, and how her love affair literally precipitated annexation of Mandalay and Northern Burma by the British. Miss Tennyson-Jesse's *The Story of Burma* (Macmillan 1946), though lacking the surrealist romance of the *The Lacquer Lady*, is nevertheless an excellent historical study of Burma up to the Second World War. (Written while the Japanese were still in occupation, the final chapter asks 'What next?'.)

E C V Foucar lived in Burma as a child and later, until the Japanese invasion in 1942, as a barrister. Of his extensive writings about the country, *Mandalay the Golden* (Dobson 1963) is perhaps his most lively.

As for history books, the most helpful and interesting include *The Pagoda War* by A T Q Stewart (Faber 1972), which deals with the Anglo-Burmese conflicts of the mid-19th century; *Stilwell and the American Experience in China* by Barbara Tuchman (Macmillan 1971); *The Making of Burma* by Dorothy Woodman (Cresset Press 1962); *The Stricken Peacock* by the Burmese historian, Maung Htin Aung (Martinus Nijhoff 1965); and *A History of Modern Burma* by J F Cady (Cornell University Press 1958).

Of the numerous biographies written on the Second World War *The Road Past Mandalay* by John Masters (Michael Joseph 1962) and *A Hell of a Licking: the Retreat from Burma 1941−2* by James Lunt (Collins 1986) are excellent.

Two books which afford the reader a unique insight into Burmese family life and philosophy are by the renowned Burmese authoress, Mi Mi Khaing. The first, *The Burmese Family* (Longman 1946, A M S Press New York 1984) is dedicated to her 'Father and Mother' who have 'shown to five children the shining path of moderation that is the Middle Way', so through her sensistive and lyrical prose Daw Mi Khaing reveals the path of the Middle Way to the reader. In the second book *Cook and Entertain the Burmese Way* (Daw Ma Ma Khin 1975, available in Burma) the secrets of the Burmese housewife are vouchsafed. Daw Mi Mi Khaing, a university lecturer, has recently published a book on the role of women in Burmese society entitled *World of Burmese Woman* (Zed Books 1984).

There are currently available two other English-language guide books dealing with the country as a whole: *Burma: a travel survival kit* (Lonely Planet 1979), and the *Insight Guide to Burma* (Apa Production 1981), as well as two English-language picture books; *Burma the Golden* (Apa 1982) and Caroline Courtauld's *In Search of Burma* (Shangri-la Press, Hong Kong and Frederick Muller London, 1984). Several interesting books for the traveller are published in Burma. The *Pictorial Guide to Pagan*, compiled by the Director of Burma's Archaeological Survey; *The Golden Glory: Shwedagon Pagoda*, compiled by the Directorate of Information; and *Historical Sites in Burma* by Aung Thau. For the lacquerware enthusiast, there is a beautiful book entitled *Burmese Lacquerware* by Sylvia Fraser-Lu (Tamarind Press, Bangkok 1985). Finally, there are Dr Htin Aung's excellent handbooks which help one get under the skin of Burmese culture. Some of these have recently been republished in Burma including *Burmese Law Tales*, *Burmese Folk Tales*, *Burmese Drama*, and *Folk Elements in Burmese Buddhism*.

Hotels

The recent increase in tourist arrivals in Burma has put a severe strain on room availability throughout the country during the peak tourist season of November to March.

There are only eight establishments totalling 400 rooms open to foreigners in Rangoon. Of these eight, only four — The Inya Lake, The Strand, Thamada and Kandawgyi Hotels — meet what might be described as the minimum standards acceptable to the average foreign tourist. Of these four, the venerable Strand Hotel (see page 95) dating from the turn-of-the-century British Burma is without question the most 'interesting' if not luxurious. The Inya Lake, built by the Soviets in the mid 1960s, lacks both the central location and the old-world charm of the Strand, being a sort of neo-Stalinist version of the Holiday Inn. Outside of Rangoon, the beautiful Thiripyitsaya Hotel in Pagan is a truly lovely adaptation of traditional Burmese styles and modern comfort. In fact, this establishment is by far the finest accommodation available in the country. Elsewhere, the word 'hotel' does not really apply to the hostelries on offer. Guest houses, as they are, range in quality of comfort and service from terrible to fair, but in all cases the good-natured attention of their Burmese staff makes up for what they lack in creature comforts.

Hotels owned by the Hotel and Tourist Corporation

Prices current as of March 1987

Region/Hotels	Rooms	Superior US$	Standard US$	Economy US$
Rangoon				
Inya Lake	single	30	23	—
	double	33.50	26.50	—
Strand	single	23	17.50	11.50
	double	26.50	21	14
Thamada	single	20	18	—
	double	23	20	—
Sakantha	single	—	12	—
	double	—	14	—
Kandawgyi	single	29	*17.50/15.50	—
	double	29	*21/17.50	—
Dagon	single	—	6	3.50
	double	—	7	6
Garden Guest House	single	—	7	3.50
	double	—	9.50	6
YMCA	single	6.40	3.20	—
	double	7.20	4.80	—

Pagan

Thiripyitsaya	single	18.50	—	—
	double	24.50	—	—
Irra Inn	single	—	6	2.50
	double	—	7	3.50

Mandalay

Mandalay Hotel	single	23	14	8
	double	23	17.50	10
Mya Mandala	single	—	7	6
	double	—	9.50	7

Maymyo

Nan Myaing	single	10	7.50	—
	double	17	9	—
Maymyo Inn	single	—	—	4.50
	double	—	—	6.50

Taunggyi

Taunggyi Hotel	single	23	11.50/9.50	—
	double	23	15/11.50	—
Inle Inn	single	—	11.50/9.50	—
	double	—	15/11.50	—

Kalaw

Kalaw Hotel	single	—	7	3.50
	double	—	9.50	5

Sandoway

Ngapali Beach Hotel	single	—	9.50	—
	double	—	11.50	—

(open from October to mid-May only)

Note: — Rates indicated are subject to ten percent service charges.
— Visitors may also stay at the Hostel in Rangoon and registered Private Guest Houses with minimal facilities and common bath at Pagan, Mandalay and Taunggyi.
* Lake view

Restaurants

Owing to the relative lack of refrigeration and imported ingredients, Burma is most definitely not a gourmet's paradise. Furthermore, hygiene is generally not up to standard and the foreign tourist cannot be too cautious when eating from both the street-side stalls or the better hotel restaurants (hepatitis is so prevalent that a gamma globulin shot before visiting is highly recommended). In recent years, however, several relatively good restaurants have established themselves in Rangoon. Below is a list of four which have been tried and tested and found to be considerably better than average.

In Mandalay, the **Shan Cherry Restaurant** was that city's best until it was destroyed by fire in 1985, and it has recently been re-established.

For beverages, Mandalay Beer, Mandalay Rum and Mandalay Brandy stand alone in the alcoholic drinks department (that is, of course, legally available). The rum is actually very good, the beer varies bottle to bottle. There are several locally produced soft drinks, some of which, like the lime soda, can be quite refreshing. Tea and coffee, both Burmese in origin, are the most commonly consumed beverages.

Rangoon

Ruby's
50 Spark Street
tel. 71106

Good Chinese food, but the decor and cleanliness leave something to be desired. Two blocks from the Strand. Try the steamed crab claws.

Yin Swe
137 University Avenue
tel. 30361

Good Chinese food. A clean, well-lit place. There is also an air-conditioned private dining room that can be reserved in advance. Try the shark's fin soup.

Go by taxi. It is between the centre of town and Inya Lake Hotel.

Burma Kitchen
141 Shwegondaing Road
tel. 50493

Good Burmese and Chinese food. Clean and air-conditioned. Try the Burmese specialities.

Go by taxi. Between the centre of town and the Inya Lake Hotel.

Mya Kan Tha
70 Natmauk Lanthwe (corner of Po Sein Road)
tel. 52712

One of the better Chinese restaurants, the Mya Kan Tha is located in a large mansion in one of the better parts of town. Try the seafood.
Go by taxi.

Index of Places